Beyond the
Fairy Tale

Dr. Missy T. Kifetew

Contents

Dedicated to my only daughter, Lydia, who always shows me the beauty of thinking outside the box.

My daughter, not only do I love and adore you, but I always pray for you—for God to finish what He's already started in you.

Introduction

When you look around, read magazines or books, or watch TV shows and movies, you might get the idea that sex is something everybody is doing everywhere, with anybody, at any time. Most media promotes a message that sex is harmless and fun, something for everyone to play and experiment with—with anyone, anywhere, anytime. Big-name Hollywood stars are doing it; half your friends at school are doing it (or at least it seems like they are); even the people on billboards are doing it. Anything that comes against this Hollywood view may feel like it is fighting against your freedom to have pleasure and joy.

But nothing is further from the truth. In a TV show or a movie, the actors may look as if they're having the maximum joy and happiness a person can have in this life through their sexual "freedom"—but they are just acting. It's a movie, not real life. The truth is very different from what we see portrayed on TV, billboards, and gossip columns.

Sex is a part of who we are. We all are the product of sex, after all! There is nothing wrong with sex or with people who are having sex. No, the problem is not sex—*the problem is having sex outside of marriage.* In addition to the shame and regret sex outside marriage brings to life, it is the cause of unintended pregnancies, sexually transmitted diseases, interference with things like school, career plans, and friendships, and insecurity and broken hearts. All these problems sometimes result from not knowing and understanding the plan and purpose of God regarding sex.

But wait. Purpose and plan? God? God knows about sex?

Yes! God is the One who created sex, and God doesn't create anything without a purpose or plan. He has a purpose and plan for you, and he sure has a purpose and plan for sex too. Invite God to be involved in all areas of your life, including your sexuality. Separating God and our sexual life is like a double whammy: Life will be hell on earth apart from the help and guidance of God, and sex without God brings agony, despair, fear, and even death.

So if there is a purpose and plan for sex, where can you find it?

I'm from a very large family, and sex was one of the "forbidden" topics none of us dared to talk about. I didn't know where to find the truth, so I began to explore. I used all the trial-and-error techniques I could think of to find answers to my countless questions. As you can imagine, I was looking for answers in all the wrong places. And to tell you the truth, with all the possibilities of contracting life-threatening sexually transmitted diseases which are the most likely results of sexually promiscuous lifestyles, I praise God that I'm still alive and well.

In hindsight, I can see how my life would have been different had I have known what I know now back then. I can't change my past, but I *can* inform other girls of what I know about sex so that they won't make the same mistakes I did when I was young.

My husband and I have been married now almost eighteen years, and we are blessed with three wonderful kids—two boys and one girl. Our beautiful daughter just turned fourteen. As she was celebrating her tenth birthday, embarking into adolescence and trying to fit in with her friends at school, I started to worry about her and the choices she might make in her life.

I started looking for all the opportunities I could get to be alone with her so we could chat about anything that was on her mind. Then I thought that reading a book with her might be the way to communicate about sex. Since we both love reading books, I decided we should read a book together about sexual purity—but I couldn't find the kind of short book I was looking for. Talented, educated, and respected Christian authors have written some wonderful books about sex and sexual purity, but none of them seemed satisfying to me.

When I couldn't find the one book I was looking for, I decided to jot down what I wanted to share with my daughter. Before I knew it, I began to find myself often in front of my laptop, typing and retyping the things I thought important to share. And when I was finished with all my points, I thought this would be a great resource for any young Christian girl who wants to pursue a sexually pure life. Remember, I know what it's like to feel like you can't find the answers! So I decided to make my notes into a book.

The first two chapters of this book show you the two basic necessities I believe you need in order to pursue a sexually pure life. These are a personal relationship with the Lord Jesus Christ and an attitude and character that is honoring and respecting toward your parents.

The next three chapters are designed to help you see the beauty of God's creation in your sexuality. They will look at biology and help you understand how you have been designed.

The rest of the book directly addresses sexual purity. We will turn to the great "user's manual" for our lives, which is the Bible. In the Bible, we find the Creator of sex, and we find the purpose and plan for sex and God's instructions about it. When you know why sex was created, what purpose God created it for, and why it is only good for you when it happens in marriage, you will treasure it as it is treasured by God. And of course, you will be a partaker of the pleasure of sex as God created it to be!

This is my desire for you, precious daughter of God: that you, at a young age, will know about sex according to the Word of God so that you will be one of those privileged people who experiences the true, authentic, lasting joy and pleasure of sex, and spares your life from the consequences of sex outside of marriage. What you know and what you don't know about sex can make a big difference in your life—like the difference between darkness and light.

The last chapter contains commonly asked questions in the area of sex—questions other preteens, teens, and twenty-something-year-olds are asking. If you have a question that is not addressed in this chapter, please send me your question via e-mail at CG-STATNOW@gmail.com.

As you read this book, I invite you to join the CG-STAT program. CG-STAT stands for Chosen Girls for Such a Time As This. You can visit the website, www.appealforpurity.org, read the blog and articles, and watch videos on the topic of sexual purity. Your parents and youth leaders can download the Leader's Guide and Parent's Guide along with the book so that you will get the full benefit of this program by launching a group study together, helping you find other girls who share your moral values and want a life of sexual purity just like you do. It's wonderful and energizing to seek purity together! I believe this program will help you know the truth and be equipped to fight back against the lies the devil, the world, and the flesh will throw your way.

Jesus says: "The Truth will set you free" (John 8:32).

Yes, the Truth will set you free!

As you read *Beyond the Fairy Tale,* you will find one fact

repeatedly coming to you, and that fact is this: Life for the most part is a matter of choice. There are things that can happen to us because of others and/or natural circumstances, but there are lots of things in life we can choose—for example, we can choose between regret for seeking a quick fix or peace and joy for seeking lasting pleasure in life.

Jesus said, "I have come that they may have life, and have it to the full" (John 10:10).

Abundant or full life is what Jesus wants to give to each one of us. This book will show you how you make that kind of life yours for free, without any strings attached.

CHAPTER ONE

❧

Basic Necessity #1: Relationship with Jesus

Sofia was eighteen years old when I met her. She told me that she began dating when she was seventeen. She dated a young man for two months, and he called it quits after he slept with her. She didn't know the reason, and she couldn't reach him after that. When she told me about this incident, I thought she wanted someone to comfort her—but that was not it. As I sat down with her for more than fifteen minutes, I realized that after she broke up with the first young man, she couldn't stop herself from going out and sleeping with different men. And she told me, "I want to stop this life, but I can't."

Then I asked her, "Sophia, what have you tried to do to stop this vicious circle of going in and coming out of relationships?"

She looked at me sorrowfully and said, "I keep on telling myself never to do it again, but I always find myself in it and I don't know what to do. Maybe I need to have a stronger willpower."

"Sofia, do you know that the life you are trying to live is something you can't do by willpower?" I asked.

A sense of relief changed her sad face into something beautiful, and she asked, "I can't?"

I answered, "No, you can't. And as a matter of fact, none of us can. You are trying to lead a sexually pure life, but none of us can pursue sexual purity without the strength of someone who can help us do that."

"What is a sexually pure life, and who is the person who can help me live like that?" Sofia asked.

Sexual purity can be defined as keeping your life free of any sexual activity or sexual pursuits outside of marriage. Sexual purity is the standard of God, the teaching of the Bible to keep people from hurting themselves or others.

Sexual purity is not the standard of this world.

You don't have to look too far to learn about the world's standard of sexual purity. Looking around, hearing story after story, and watching all the TV shows and movies out there, sexual purity may sound like a story of old—one of those "once upon a time" stories that has nothing to do with us now. Some people sincerely believe that there is no such thing as sexual purity in today's society. However, sexual purity is not just a story of old, and there *are* people today who lead sexually pure lives, both guys and girls who are committed to following God's design for sex.

Sexual purity is not something that just happens to a person. It is an intentional lifestyle, purposely and consciously chosen on a daily basis. It is not a one-time deal but a day to day endeavor that may require discipline and consistency.

Because sexual purity is a commitment that takes real work, there are two basic life necessities you'll need first. These are important for you to have to be able to pursue a sexually pure life. They are:

1. Having or deepening a personal relationship with the Lord Jesus Christ
2. Honoring and respecting your parents

These are the two fundamentals upon which you will be able to build a sexually pure life.

A Personal Relationship with Christ Jesus

Jesus Christ made a way for us to have a whole new kind of relationship with God—a kind that changes our lives from the inside out. You see, in Old Testament times before Jesus came, people had to do the commandments of God in order for them to have fellowship with God.

Here is the summary of the first commandments God gave to his people through Moses. (They are known as the Ten Commandments, and you can read the details of them in Exodus 20.)

1. You shall have no other gods before me.
2. You shall not make for yourself an idol.
3. You shall not take the name of the Lord your God in vain
4. Remember the Sabbath day to keep it holy.
5. Honor your father and your mother, that your days may be long upon the land which the Lord your God is giving you.
6. You shall not murder.
7. You shall not commit adultery.
8. You shall not steal.
9. You shall not bear false witness against your neighbor.
10. You shall not covet your neighbor's possession.

These commandments and many more were given to the people of Israel through Moses. They were requirements in order for them to be qualified to be with God in total peace and harmony. However, no one has ever gotten to that perfection on his or her own, because from the beginning, Adam sinned against God, and we all inherited Adam's sinful nature. It was (and still is) impossible for anyone to keep those commandments with perfection, so no human being could be found worthy enough to be with God.

God loves the people he created, and he wants to fellowship with all of us, but he can't fellowship with sin or with a heart that is full of sin.

God is holy, and he demands holiness in us. He loves us and desires to fellowship with us—but not with our sin and sinful nature. For God to bring us back to his love, he sent his Son, Jesus Christ, to die on the cross for all of our sins—from Adam's sin to the last sin of the last person who will ever live—because the wages of sin is death. God gave his Son as a payment for our sin so that he could buy (redeem) us all back to himself.

For the wages of sin is death, but the gift of God is eternal life in Christ Jesus our Lord. (Romans 6:23)

Through Christ's death, forgiveness of sin and grace to live a life that is pleasing to God have been given by God to all who believe and accept this truth.

To those who accept and believe this truth, God gives the right to be his sons and daughters, as the Bible says:

Yet to all who did receive him [Jesus], to those who believed in his name [in Jesus's name], he [God] gave the right to become children of God. (John 1:12)

For God so loved the world that he gave his one and only son, that whoever believes in him shall not perish but have eternal life. (John 3:16)

Notice one important thing here. God's commandments are not cancelled by Jesus, but Jesus kept them all on our behalf and died on the cross as a pure lamb for all of our sin. He rose from the dead and lives forever so that we can live with him. He became sin so that those who believe in him become God's righteousness. The Bible says that God credited Jesus' righteousness to those who believe in Jesus.

> God made him [Jesus] who had no sin to be sin for us, so that in him [Jesus] we might become the righteousness of God. (2 Corinthians 5:21)

> He was delivered over to death for our sins and was raised to life for our justification. (Romans 4:25)

Now, today, Jesus lives in those who trust in him. His spirit, the spirit of God, helps them live in a way that is pleasing to God, because apart from his help, it is impossible to live a life that God finds acceptable and pleasing. This is why knowing and loving Jesus is the first necessity for living a sexually pure life: Without his help, it can't be done!

It's also important that we don't try to be sexually pure because we want to be "good enough" to be loved by God. We are already loved! Those who belong to Jesus want to please Jesus by obeying his words, not so that they can be with him, but because they already *are* with him. He loves them first; they love him back by obeying his words. If they sin against him, knowingly or unknowingly, through the confession of their sin they will receive his forgiveness, again through the work of Christ on the cross.

Jesus is a gift from God for all people, but only those who believe and receive this truth can enjoy the eternal life that is found only in him.

> For God so loved the world that he gave his one and only
> son, that whoever believes in him shall not perish but have
> eternal life. (John 3:16)

> Yet to all who did receive him [Jesus], to those who believed
> in his name [in Jesus's name], he [God] gave the right to
> become children of God. (John 1:12)

When Jesus was on the earth, he gave a brand-new command-ment to his followers. That commandment is for us to love God and others through the love that pours down into our life when we believe in the Son of God, Jesus Christ.

> A new command I give you: Love one another. As I have loved
> you, so you must love one another. By this everyone will know
> that you are my disciples, if you love one another. (John 13:34–35)

> God's love has been poured out into our hearts through the
> Holy Spirit, who has been given to us. (Romans 5:5)

Jesus' disciples asked Jesus what they needed to do to have eternal life, and this is what he said to them:

> Then they asked him, "What must we do to do the works
> God requires?" Jesus answered, "The work of God is this: to
> believe in the one he has sent." (John 6:28–29)

If you have come across this truth for the first time and want to invite Christ into your heart, seize this moment to make that change in your heart and pray this prayer with me:

Dear heavenly Father, I come to you in the name
of your son, Jesus Christ. Thank you for sending your son,
Jesus Christ, to die on the cross for my sin. I am a sinner,
and I accept your forgiveness through your son. Lord Jesus,
I invite you to come and live in my heart. I accept you as
my personal Lord and Savior. Lord, please help me live a
life that brings glory and honor to you. From this day
forward, I will follow you. Help me to do just that.
I pray this in the name of Jesus Christ, amen.

God himself, through his son, Jesus Christ, will help you lead
a life that is sexually pure. Apart from him, we can do nothing, as
the Bible says:

I am the vine; you are the branches. If you remain in me and
I in you, you will bear much fruit; *apart from me you can do
nothing.* (John 15:5, emphasis added)

If you have already received Jesus Christ as your personal Lord
and Savior, continue to deepen your relationship with him. Seek
him through praying every day, studying his words in the Bible,
and fellowshipping with his spirit and other believers through
going to church regularly and participating there.

Seek to know your God more than last year or the year before.
Just because you received Jesus Christ as your personal Lord and
Savior four years ago doesn't mean that you are Jesus' follower in
your everyday life. Strive to grow in his Word, the Bible, so that
you will live in his Spirit. As you surrender to the teachings of
God's Word, the Word itself helps you live a life that is pleasing to
God and fulfilling to you.

Life Principle:

"Because God has made us for Himself, our hearts are restless until they rest in Him." Augustine of Hippo

The desire to be good enough without God is just a fantasy because there is no goodness outside God.

> I am the vine; you are the branches. If you remain in me and I in you, you will bear much fruit; *apart from me you can do nothing.* (John 15:5, emphasis added)

Assignment:

The assignments given in this book can be done individually or together with your CG-STAT group.

Did you receive Christ as your personal Lord and Savior? If you did, write down what happened in a journal; or, if you are in a CG-STAT group, share your story in the next class.

CHAPTER TWO

Basic Necessity #2: Honoring Your Parents

Sara was a fourteen-year-old young girl. She has a contagious smile and a wonderful attitude. After I gave teaching to her group on sexual purity, she stayed behind to ask me the most common question I get from teenagers: "Do you think I'm old enough to date?"

"Before I tell you what I think, I want to know what your parents think about that," I said.

She smiled and answered, "Both my parents are just high school graduates." Rolling both her eyes, she continued, "And they both are from 'that generation,' if you know what I mean."

"No, I don't know what you mean," I said.

She reluctantly said, "Well, they have no clue about this life."

I pulled out two chairs and asked her to sit. But Sara was not willing to sit down and talk about this. Instead she said, "You know what, I have to run now. I will message you later on your Facebook page." And she disappeared. I've never heard from her again.

Whenever this issue comes up, I always remember Sara. It is my prayer that she finds someone to tell her about the truth of God I'm about to discuss with you: honoring your parents. Actually, honoring your parents is the second basic thing you need to have to help you seek a sexually pure life.

Do you know in the Ten Commandments of God, only one was given with promise attached to it? Yep, that is commandment number five. Here is how it reads in two of the Old Testament books:

> Honor your father and your mother, *so that you may live long in the land the* LORD *your God is giving you.* (Exodus 20:12, emphasis added)

> Honor your father and your mother, as the LORD your God has commanded you, *so that you may live long and that it may go well with you in the land the* LORD *your God is giving you.* (Deuteronomy 5:16, emphasis added)

Today, as I already shared, we live in a brand-new commandment that calls us to love God and love others with the love that is lavishly poured down in our lives when we trust Christ as our personal Lord and Savior. Here is what Jesus said about the new commandment:

> A new command I give you: Love one another. As I have loved you, so you must love one another. By this everyone will know that you are my disciples, if you love one another. (John 13:34–35)

However, once you let Christ live in your heart, he helps you keep all the old *and* new commandments of God. This is not so you can be called a daughter of God, but so the world will know that you *are* a daughter of God! Because of this, when you keep God's commandments, all the promises of God belong to you. Yes, they do!

For no matter how many promises God has made, *they are
"Yes" in Christ*. And so through him the "Amen" is spoken by
us to the glory of God." (2 Corinthians 1:20, emphasis added)

You see, the promises of God are eternal. His Word lives forever! Jesus said, " Heaven and earth will pass away, but my words
will never pass away" (Mark 13:31).

That means the command with a promise also stays true forever. You can't live a long life and enjoy health, success, and happiness while dishonoring and disrespecting your parents. That is
just impossible.

Honoring and respecting your parents is a very basic spiritual discipline that is necessary for you to live a healthy life. That
includes living a sexually pure life. In fact, because parents have
more experience and wisdom than their children do, and because
they usually want to protect and help them, honoring your parents can be *especially* powerful to help you live a sexually pure life.
Respecting and honoring them is like building a strong foundation upon which you can build the rest of your life.

Maybe this sounds fishy to you. Maybe you doubt that honoring your parents can really be very important. Your parents may
not seem to know that much about life or the things that are important to you. They may not have a college degree, or they might not
have an important and rich family background. You might not
always be proud to talk about your family background. But one
thing is for sure, they are your parents.

Notice: The command (not suggestion) to honor your parents
doesn't have a condition. It doesn't say, "If your parents have at
least a diploma or a degree, they are worthy of your respect" or
"Honor your parents only if they're cool like your friend's parents."

No, it doesn't say that. There is only one criterion for you to respect your parents. And that is that they are your parents. You didn't choose your parents, and they didn't choose you. It was God who chose your parents for you and you for them. And God is always right in everything he does. He has never made a mistake, and he will never make one in the future. When you respect your parents, you are respecting and honoring God, who bestowed the authority of parenthood on your parents.

Notice one more thing: When the Bible says "honor your parents," it doesn't mean that you can disrespect and dishonor other people. No!

Rather, it means that if you respect the two most important people in your life, the people who brought you into this world, it will be very easy for you to respect God and others.

When I was a teenager, the one rule that was very difficult for me to accept and live by was my parents' late-night curfew. When I was a senior in high school, I thought I was the most unfortunate girl because I had to go home on Friday night before dusk. Some of the girls I knew were allowed to stay out however long they wanted to. Some of them just disobeyed their parents.

I wanted to disobey my parents, but I was very scared of my dad. On Mondays, I used to hear about all sorts "fun stuff" the other girls did on Friday nights. However, I didn't know that staying those extra late hours was costing some of those girls their dignity when they were asked or forced to sleep with the men they stayed late with.

And I never knew that those men who noticed me going home early had more respect for me than they did for the girls who were willing to stay with them.

You see, as a teen, nobody put those things together to show me that I was living under the protection of God by honoring my parents' curfew and that I was actually honoring God when I honored my parents' curfew.

Oh, how I wish I had continued to honor and respect my parents' curfew until the end! But I didn't. I rebelled in my own way, and I paid the price for it as I went through the guilt and regret of failed relationships that shouldn't have happened in the first place.

Yes, when you respect the most important people in your life, your parents, you are actually honoring yourself as a person, but above all, you are honoring God who said, "Honor your mother and father." When you live under your parents' rules, including time curfews, you are showing that you are honoring your parents, God, yourself, and others as you don't expect them to dishonor their parents. When you honor your parents and their rules, hear this: You are also respecting the man you will marry as you save yourself for him.

Life Principle:

"Be faithful in small things because it is in them that your strength lies." (Mother Teresa)

Practicing honoring and respecting your parents is like taking a baby step toward respecting others outside your home. If you respect your parents, you won't have a hard time respecting your school rules and regulations. When you grow up and have a job, you won't struggle to respect your boss and the rules of the company you work for. If you are faithful in smaller things (in this case respecting your parents), you will be faithful in bigger things (in this case, respecting others); if you are not faithful in smaller things, you will not be faithful in bigger things.

Whoever can be trusted with very little can also be trusted with much, and whoever is dishonest with very little will also be dishonest with much. (Luke 16:10, emphasis added)

This world is full of different people. When you become independent, you will meet all types of people in different settings. For you to be successful in life, you will need people skills—skills that include the wisdom and knowledge to know how to live with others in harmony. Respecting and honoring your parents is a key foundational characteristic you need to develop now.

Remember this: People who respect others, including God and their parents, respect themselves too. When they respect themselves and others, they will choose a life that will bring honor and respect for themselves, others, and most importantly God. They will tend not to be attracted to a sexually-perverted lifestyle, which degrades a person to nothingness.

Life Principle:

"Your attitude, not your aptitude, will determine your altitude." (Zig Ziglar)

Your parents might never have gone to school or earned a degree, but they have walked on this earth longer than you have. That means they have more knowledge than you when it comes to what can be dangerous or beneficial for you. Likewise, your parents may not seem "cool" or know all about the latest clothes or toys or lingo, but they have deep wisdom from years past that they can share with you.

Listen, my son, to your father's instruction
and do not forsake your mother's teaching.

They are a garland [a wreath of flowers] to grace your head
and a chain to adorn your neck. (Proverbs 1:8–9)

The fruits of honoring and respecting your parents can't
be counted or measured. They are priceless. God will reward
you throughout your life, as he promised in his Word. Those
rewards come in different forms and shapes, such as health,
well-being, a sexually-pure life, success in things you do, fulfillment, contentment, and more. If you choose not to honor and
respect your parents, the opposite may come true in your life.

Life Principle:
Whatever you sow, you shall reap!

Do not be deceived: God cannot be mocked. A man [or
woman] reaps what he [or she] sows. Whoever sows to please
their flesh, from the flesh will reap destruction; whoever
sows to please the Spirit, from the Spirit will reap eternal life.
(Galatians 6:7–8)

Know this: Respecting your parents may sound good and
easy, but it is not easy for our flesh to do it! Because of Adam's
fall, we all fall short of the glory of God. That means we can't obey
the Word of God unless God's spirit helps us to do it. That is why,
first and foremost, you need to have a personal relationship with
the Lord Jesus Christ for you to be able to honor and respect your
parents and be the person God created you to be.

These two life necessities, receiving the Lord Jesus Christ as
your Lord and personal Savior and honoring your parents, will
anchor you to the truth. It will be hard to shake you off of the truth

and God's blessings that come with it! Rather than you trying to follow God's blessings, God's blessings will follow you. When a storm of life comes, since your life is established on a strong foundation, you will stand strong.

Read what Jesus says:

> Therefore everyone who hears these words of mine and puts them into practice is like a wise man who built his house on the rock. The rain came down, the streams rose, and the winds blew and beat against that house; yet it did not fall, because it had its foundation on the rock. But everyone who hears these words of mine and does not put them into practice is like a foolish man who built his house on sand. The rain came down, the streams rose, and the winds blew and beat against that house, and it fell with a great crash. (Matthew 7:24–27)

Life Principle:

One will have respect for self and others only after he/she first learns how to respect his/her parents.

Assignment:

The assignments given in this book can be done individually or together with your CG-STAT group.

1. Sara is a 16-year-old girl. She wants to pray immediately after she gets to school but her parents don't allow her to do that. What do you think Sara needs to do in that situation?

2. Write down practical ways you express honor and respect to your parents. If you are part of CG-STAT group, share your ways with the group.

3. Read again the life principle in this chapter and write down

how you understood it in light of what else you read from the chapter. If you are part of the CG-STAT group, share with your group your thoughts and understandings.

⚘

CHAPTER THREE

The Dawn of Sexuality

The Bible says in the beginning the earth was covered by water; it was formless, shapeless, and dark, but the spirit of God was hovering over it (Genesis 1:2). Then God began speaking all things into existence by calling them. He called light, different water bodies, the earth and the sky, plants, the moon and the sun, stars and galaxies, and living creatures that live on land and in the water. He created all these things within five days. Then on the sixth day of creation, God created more animals and creatures that live on the ground. Then God said, "Let us make mankind in our image, in our likeness" (Genesis 1:26).

But notice one thing here: God spoke everything else into existence, but not the man! God made the man with his own hands. After he made Adam, he took a rib out of Adam and fashioned Eve—again with his own hands. Then God brought Eve to Adam, just like a father brings his daughter to her husband during a wedding ceremony, and he gave her to him so that they would be husband and wife—so that they would be one.

In order for Adam and Eve to become one, God created in them sexual desire: physical and sexual attraction to one another. Even today, that attraction brings men and women together and makes them one. And after God saw all the creation and how he made the two become one through sexual union, the Bible says that "it was very good."

Goodness is part of God's nature. He is good, and all he does is good. In the book of Genesis, after every day of creation, we read one statement: "And God saw that it was good." Creation took seven days, and we read this same statement seven times in the first chapter of Genesis. But it's only after the sixth day of creation that this same statement is stated in a little different way. It says, "God saw all that he had made, and it was *very good*" (Genesis 1:31b, emphasis added).

But notice that God didn't create a little-boy Adam or a little-girl Eve. Both were created fully grown. That means they didn't have to go through the growing process called puberty.

I know, many of you are probably thinking at this point, "I wish that was the case with me! Puberty is so gross, and I wish I could just marry the first boy I fall in love with."

But remember, *everything* God created is good, and the process of puberty, which you and I have to go through to get to sexual maturity, is "very good." We can agree with God about that! However, this sexual maturity doesn't happen overnight. It takes time, and it sometimes takes a toll on us. We're developing fast and hard, and that can drive us crazy at times!

To understand God's plan for sex, you have to start at the beginning. So let's briefly talk about this process of maturity.

Puberty is the process of physical change by which your body matures toward sexual reproduction. During this process, your body matures into an adult body, a body which is capable of duplicating itself in the sexual reproduction process.

For girls, the dawn of puberty begins around the age of eleven or twelve when a hormonal signal from the brain is sent to your ovaries where eggs are formed. (Eggs are necessary to make babies—it is sperm in the case of boys.)

This signal initiates the whole process of puberty. From that time, your body will start to go through a lot of changes, including general body growth. Your breasts will develop, and you'll notice new hair growth in areas such as under your arms and in your pubic area (your sexual organ area).

The number-one mark of puberty is the start of your menstrual cycle. (Yes, I know—this is the gross part!) You will experience a flow of blood out of your sexual organ for at least three days every twenty-eight to thirty days. This is a process that will continue until you are in your fifties. It stops throughout pregnancy and resumes after the birth of the baby.

The menstrual cycle occurs every month as the body "builds a house" for the baby it is expecting to raise if an egg gets fertilized by a sperm in that time. When that doesn't happen, the brain automatically sends signals to destroy the house that was built for the baby, and this results in the flow of blood. (This is a very simplified way of explaining the process—the actual process is amazing and detailed, and you can learn more about it if you study science.) Your menstrual cycle (also known as your period) is one of the signs to let you know that you are not a little girl any more. You are maturing into a woman.

During your menstrual cycle, good hygiene is important. You have to use menstrual pads or tampons so the blood won't leak. It is very important that you keep on changing your menstrual pads or tampons frequently. After you finish your period cycle, it's a good idea to carry at least one pad in your bag or purse, in case of emergency or until you get used to the timing of your cycle!

Whether you are in your menstrual cycle or not, it is always good to keep your sexual organ area clean with a moisturized, scent-free soap. Avoid also doing things such as douching (using a jet or current of water) at all times since your sexual organ area doesn't need that aggressive way of cleaning.

If you're still at an age where your parents have been telling you when to shower or even helping you do that, puberty means it's time for a change. Now you shouldn't wait until your parents tell you to take a shower or brush your teeth. It is your sole responsibility to take a shower, use deodorant, clean your bedroom, change your underclothes, and clean up after yourself on a daily basis.

Regular exercise and healthy eating habits are very important for your health since your body has a tendency to get bigger than it is supposed to. Obesity can become a problem at this age. Obesity can be a source of all sicknesses, including diabetic, cancer, and heart problems, and it can also cause emotional sicknesses such as anxiety or depression. Some girls also suffer from an obsessive desire to be skinny. This strong desire drives these girls into different eating disorders, which can become serious and debilitating illnesses such as anorexia and bulimia.

Assignment:

The assignments given in this book can be done individually or together with your CG-STAT group.

If you notice changes in your body or character other than what you read on this chapter, discuss it with your parents. If you are part of the CG-STAT group and feel comfortable sharing that with the class, it will be a good discussion point for the whole class.

CHAPTER FOUR

"I Think I'm a Bad Girl"

When Grace came to me, she had celebrated her thirteenth birthday a week earlier. I said to her, "Happy-belated birthday!" She gave me a quick smile and said, "Thank you!"

From her look, I knew something was wrong. So I asked her if she wanted to talk about it. She quickly said, "Yes, but I hope you will understand me."

Not knowing what to expect, I said, "I will try my best. I guess I once celebrated my thirteenth birthday too, so I will try to find a way to relate with you."

She said, "You know that I have two best friends?"

I said, "I know them well."

She said, "Well, I think we are becoming very different people these days. Both my friends care a lot about school, and they always talk about school and what class they need to study more to keep their A+ grade. Don't get me wrong, I care about my school too, but these days, I feel like I'm starting to drift away from life and becoming a person I don't want to be."

I said, "What kind of person are you becoming?"

"I want to hang out with the boys in our class. I talk to them a lot, and I enjoy the time I spend with them. I also love to watch those romantic movies and . . ."

She stopped as if she was very scared to say the next sentence. I immediately said to her, ". . . and you dream about having one of those boys as a boyfriend or something like that?"

She opened her mouth as if to say something like, "No, that is not it." Instead, pushing her shoulders down, she exhaled with some relief and said, "Yes. But none of my friends has that kind of dream."

I asked her, "Oh, so you asked them and they said they had never had that kind of dream?"

She said, "No, I didn't ask them, but I know that they are good girls and they don't think or dream like that."

"Are you saying that you are a bad girl?" I asked.

"Compared to them, I think. Don't you think so?" She continued to study my face to get the answer from my face, not just my mouth.

I just laughed. She wanted to laugh with me, but she was hesitant.

Grace is not the only girl who may think this way. Some girls worry thinking that they are the only ones with this kind of thought or dream. Puberty brings obvious external body or physical changes you see from the outside, but the changes of puberty are not all physical. Many will affect your mind and emotions as well. During puberty, you start to become interested in talking about boys, reading love stories, or watching romantic movies. You may dream of becoming a princess who steals the heart of Prince Charming. You become conscious of the presence of boys in your class. You may even fantasize about becoming the wife of a boy in your class or in your neighborhood, or even of a movie actor.

All of this is normal. You will also find yourself wanting to chat with boys your age. Your main topic with your friends may be who has a crush on whom; or playing a game of picking a boy you know for your future husband. You will likely also become conscious of how you look and how you dress up or style your hair. You may become eager to have a boyfriend.

It's about now that the fairy tale tends to kick in! You may find yourself flying into Dreamland City, finding Mr. Charming, and dancing with him in the center of a ballroom. Your dreamland may include you and a handsome boy chatting, laughing, dancing, and kissing. Depending on how much time you spend watching TV shows and movies, your dreamland can get to the point of picturing yourself sleeping with a boy. I will say more about how viewing inappropriate TV shows and movies leads you to sin and battles against your ability to remain sexually pure. For now, know this: If you are exposed to sexually explicit shows and movies, you will think and dream about sex.

When all of this happens, you may think, *I think I'm a bad girl for thinking this.* You may feel guilt or shame about it. But the truth of the matter is you are not bad; rather, you're normal and healthy. This change is a natural phenomenon, not a matter of being bad or good. It's what you do with your changing thoughts and emotions that ultimately counts.

Remember this: A thought passing through your mind doesn't make you sinful, but when you let a thought linger in your brain, it is just a matter of time before you are acting it out, even against your own will, beliefs, and convictions. So take caution. It is good to limit your screen time or avoid watching those shows you know for sure are not appropriate for you. The fairy tale presented by the media has a dark side, so it's wise to guard yourself against being sucked in by it!

Life Principle:

"You cannot prevent the birds of sorrow from flying over your head, but you can prevent them from building nests in your hair." (Chinese proverb)

There are things in life that you can't change or stop from happening. But other things *can* be changed or stopped. One of the things you can stop in life is a thought that may come to your mind. Do not dwell on those thoughts which are against your beliefs and convictions. Rather, find a Bible verse or something else that is true, pure, and lovely, and dwell on that instead:

Finally, brothers and sisters, whatever is true, whatever is noble, whatever is right, whatever is pure, whatever is lovely, whatever is admirable—if anything is excellent or praiseworthy—think about such things. (Philippians 4:8)

The Bible commands us to think about "good" and "praiseworthy" things. There is nothing like the Word of God itself, which is true, pure, noble, etc., to dwell on! So develop a habit of daily Bible reading and meditation ("meditation" is just taking time to think deeply about what you're reading). This will help you use the right Bible verse against the wrong thought that wants to linger in your brain. That is what Jesus did when the devil fought with him (read Matthew 4).

One of the best ways to control what you're thinking is by controlling what you're feeding your eyes, heart, and mind. Have you ever heard the saying, "Junk in, junk out"? Well, it's very true! Our brain is a very powerful organ. Sometimes it does its own things without our permission—things like ordering our hearts to beat or our lungs to inhale and exhale. But when it comes to thinking, don't forget this:

Our brain rarely creates its own things. It uses all the things we let our eyes see or our ears hear. It draws on the habits we have of thinking certain things. So watch out for yourself, even when your parents are not around. Train yourself to say "No!" to your wrong desires, like desires to watch inappropriate shows or listen to songs with offensive lyrics. If you practice saying "No" to your wrong cravings, you will save yourself from so much grief, guilt and despair.

Life Principle:
Every sin begins in the mind.

For as he (a man) thinketh in his heart, so is he. (Proverbs 23:7, KJV)

Our actions are the result of what has been processed in our minds. First we put our minds into an action, then our body parts work together to bring that action into reality. It is crucial to know what is cooking in our minds, because it is only a matter of time before the thing our mind dwells on becomes our action and lifestyle. Our brain is like the CEO of a company. It is where a decision is made, where instruction and orders are coming from. As you let your mind dwell on something, let's say being a good student, you will find it very easy to convince yourself to wake up early in the morning to study for the exam that is coming up in the following week. As you think, so are you. That's why it is very important to let your mind dwell on the things that bring forth good and praiseworthy lifestyles in your life.

Assignment:
The assignments given in this book can be done individually or together with your CG-STAT group.

Each day, read the Bible. Write down any verses that stand out to you, and spend time thinking deeply about them. If you are in a CG-STAT group, spend the first few minutes of next week's class sharing with others the Bible verse or verses you meditated on.

✣

CHAPTER FIVE

Storms of Puberty

Phoebe was twelve years old when she began complaining about her clothes. She wanted to go to the mall with her friends. She didn't want her mother to pick clothes for her. Her mother didn't allow her to go to mall with her friends because she said, "If I let her go, she'll come home with clothes she doesn't even feel comfortable wearing."

I asked Phoebe why she wanted to go with her friends.

She answered, "Because my friends don't like the clothes my mom is buying for me. All my friends are allowed to go out and buy their own clothes. Their parents drop them off at the mall and they pick their own clothes. But I am not allowed to do that."

"But your mom knows what the best outfit for you to wear is. Doesn't she?" I asked.

She replied, "She does, but my friends don't like my clothes at all; and if I don't dress like them, I can't be in their group. It is not like they will kick me out of the group, but I will be out of place."

Phoebe knew her mom could pick good clothes for her, but she wanted to buy clothes her friends approved of so that she would feel she belonged to the group. This was a sign that Phoebe was going down the tough road of peer pressure, which is one of the life stressors or storms that can hit at this time of life.

As part of the process of puberty, just like Phoebe, you may go through some life stressors or storms. The storms of puberty may not hit everyone with the same intensity or affect everybody in the same way, but they are very real.

The first one, one we all go through in one way or another and the one Phoebe is going through, is **peer pressure.** You probably already know all about this! Peer pressure is pressure from one's peers to behave in a manner similar or acceptable to them. Girls your age may want to pull you into their "group." They will do anything to convince you to join them and follow their lifestyle. Some girls may promise that you can join their "club" if you behave or dress in a certain way.

Peer pressure affects young people of all ages, from preteens to college and even beyond. As you get older, especially into junior high and high school, peer pressure can become more dangerous. Let's say the "cool girls" believe that having sex with anyone they like is okay. These girls may not consider you "cool" like them as long as you stay a virgin. (A virgin is a person who has never had sexual intercourse.)

In a situation like this, choose not to be in their group. It is better for you to be out of the club than to be in at the cost of losing your values and Christian beliefs and ending up with all kinds of regret, hurt, and misery.

Remember this: "Misery loves company." Some girls are miserable with their sexual choices and want everybody to join their unhappiness! Dare to be different. Be courageous and strong to hold your ground on what you believe. When you decide to be on the same side as God's Word, God will give you strength to stay the course. He will also reward you for your faithfulness. Don't choose the easy and quick way, no matter how much pressure there is on you to do it.

Another storm you may face as a teenager is called an **identity crisis.** An identity crisis occurs when someone doesn't know who she is, to which group she belongs, or where she wants to go in life.

The media can make an identity crisis worse by feeding you wrong ideas or lies about who you should be. Most TV shows and movies these days reward a woman who dresses up in such a way as to provoke sexual desire in men. If women expose most of their body parts, they're praised as "hot, sexy, and attractive." And yet, many shows also encourage girls to act like men. A girl who pursues a man for sex is seen by most shows and movies as the kind of girl every man will fall for. And there is some truth to that, except that not every man will fall for that kind of girl—only those who want to use and trash her.

Women are encouraged to act masculine in other ways, too. Most recent blockbuster movies promote women who can kill men without a gun, using only her hands and feet. This kind of violence is a tool the world, the devil, and the flesh use to create lust in men's hearts.

In real life, it is rare to find that kind of woman. Women can be strong and brave, but they have other God-given important roles other than being a man!

Finally, there's the lie that sleeping with anyone you want, whenever you want, is natural and fun. Most soap opera shows promote a sexually promiscuous life as a life of maximum pleasure and joy.

If a girl finds her information on who to be, how to dress up, and how to act and live from these sources, she will face an identity crisis as she forsakes the honor God bestowed on her—the honor of being loved and pursued by a guy with honor, respect, and holiness.

You see, girls have a God-given emotional desire to be loved, treasured, valued, touched, caressed, and desired. Most young single girls will have those God-given emotional desires met as they relate to their families, friends, and God. When they get married, their desires will be met as they relate to their husbands, kids, God, families, and friends. If, however, a young girl is deprived of having her emotional desires met in a healthy way, she tends to look for other outlets.

When you are tuned in to what the media is advising you to be, you can lose yourself in the middle of it. Then what you have been *created to be* and what you are becoming clash head-on, and you will have some serious identity issues.

Some girls who struggle with identity may choose to cut themselves with a blade or something sharp to relieve the stresses they feel when they find it hard to find themselves in any group. They may think that nobody loves them or cares for them because, they believe, they are ugly or something.

Remember this: Your friends, the culture, school instructors, and media may all tell you this or that regarding who you really are and why you were created. But the only message you should accept and agree with is the one you'll find in the Bible. Only the Bible says the entire truth about your identity and your purpose in life. For you to identify the truth from all the lies flying around you, it is very important that you read and study the Bible.

As a Christian, make the Bible *the* book you look at to find the truth about yourself and who you really are.

Girls in puberty and later may also face another storm, which is collectively called **eating disorders.** Bulimia and anorexia are the main eating disorders that can disrupt the life of a young woman.

Girls with bulimia eat excessively, downing a large amount of food in a very short period of time, and then try anything to get rid of what they ate—usually by vomiting or excessive exercise. These girls may have a distorted notion about their body. They tend to stand in front of the mirror and say "I'm fat" even if in reality they are not fat at all. For them, the body they see in the mirror is very fat, and they try to lose weight so that the image they see in the mirror will match the image they have in their brain. The problem is that the thinness they want to achieve has no limit. If they lose five pounds, they still think they are fat. If they lose another five pounds, they still think that they are fat. It has no end. They are fat only in their brains.

These girls try everything to lose weight. They eat too much, but they purge it all out immediately after they eat.

On the other hand, girls with anorexia avoid eating anything. Anorexia is characterized by excessive weight loss accompanied by an unrealistic fear of gaining weight. Girls with anorexia have a distorted or twisted view of their body weight. They may be thin like a stick, but they still think that they need to stay away from food to lose weight.

Remember, these girls do not get to this stage in one day. They usually start out by comparing themselves with unrealistic images, such as the airbrushed girls on a magazine cover, models, and movie actresses who actually *are* fakes—movie and camera techniques, plus excessive makeup and Photoshop, make them look the way they do. Girls may also compare themselves to a girl in their school or next door who they think has the perfect body figure they dream of having.

All of these comparisons and fears are based on a lie. You see, God created us all to be different. We have different skin colors, looks, sizes, and shapes. And regardless of our color, size, shape, or look, we are precious creatures of God.

> I praise you because I am fearfully and wonderfully made;
>   your works are wonderful, I know that full well. (Psalm 139:14)

> For we are God's masterpiece. He has created us anew in Christ Jesus, so we can do the good things he planned for us long ago. (Ephesians 2:10, NLT)

We all are God's masterpiece! You are an amazing masterpiece of God. Don't let anyone or anything tell you otherwise.

In some cases, eating disorders may result from factors other than the above. These can include family pressure, genetic or biological factors, and emotional or personality disorders. In most cases, licensed and professional help is required to help the girl who is struggling with a disorder to grasp the truth. Knowing who you are in Christ through reading and studying the Word of God is very important, but it may not be good enough to bring a solution to such challenging and complicated conditions as eating disorders. If you or someone you know suffers from these problems, find a way to take it to your parents or guardians who can seek profession help.

Another storm of life girls your age may face is **low self-esteem.** A girl with low self-esteem believes that she is not good enough, or she does not measure up beside other people's performance or looks.

Low self-esteem can be caused by many things, physical and emotional and mental. One common cause is acne. Acne is a skin condition that causes pimples or "zits" on the face and other parts of the body. Many teens deal with acne to varying degrees. If you have this condition, you can use medicine from any drug store to help get rid of the pimples. If it is severe, you may need to see your physician so that he or she can prescribe something stronger than the over-the-counter meds to get rid of the persistent zits.

Sometimes the acne condition cannot be solved in a short period of time. It may be a lifetime struggle for some. If that is the case for you, remember this: You and your life are beyond zits! You were created to live above your circumstances. Use your struggles as an instrument to make you strong so that you can comfort others who may have similar struggles.

You shouldn't let any skin condition or any condition define you. The Word of God should be the only resource you look to in order to find out who you are. No one or nothing else!

Some people struggle to accept their skin color, their hair structure, or their appearance in general. This may be because they are influenced, once again, by the media, and therefore get lost in a culture that worships a certain look or skin color. When you find yourself in Christ, you can know that you are God's masterpiece. He fashioned you in a way that is totally different from anyone else. You're very precious and unique. Your fingerprints are the only ones in this universe. Nobody has a copy of them. Why? Because you are God's masterpiece! Read and meditate on the Word of God and hide it in your heart. Then it will be very hard for anyone to convince you otherwise.

Remember this: The devil is a liar. He lied to Adam and Eve, and he continues to use the same strategy today. Once people accept his lies as truth, it is very hard to convince them otherwise. He lies to us to keep us from the blessing of God. Say "NO!" to his lies by soaking your mind, heart, and soul with the Word of God. You can't say no to the devil's lies without God's Word residing in you. It is God's Word that has authority and power over the devil's lie, not your willpower or anything else. Don't forget that!

The other thing you should put at the back of your mind is this: Satan doesn't come to your life as a beast but as an angel (read 2 Corinthians 11:12–15). He can use people or situations (including life circumstances) to lie to you. For example, if you are not careful who you choose as your friends, you will easily drift away from the truth.

So always find who you are from the Word of God. Surround yourself with people who have the same moral and spiritual values as yours, and if a situation like peer pressure or an eating disorder occurs to you, find a way to communicate that with your parents so that they seek help for you.

Life Principle:
Wrong friendship dries up the flower of the lilies of tomorrow.

Do not be misled: "Bad company corrupts good character." (1 Corinthians 15:33)

If you put a rotten tomato with a good and freshly cut tomato, what do you think would happen to those tomatoes after two days or so? Do you think the good and freshly cut tomato would be capable of making the rotten tomatoes good and fresh? I'm sure you know the answer!

In the same way, you get influenced and impacted by your surroundings more than you think or imagine. You might be a strong believer and follower of biblical teaching, including sexual purity, but if you tend to hang out with people who do not uphold the same beliefs as yours, it will be a matter of time before you forego yours and follow theirs. The best thing to do is always to surround yourself with like-minded friends: friends who uphold the values you hold dear. Their good character and attitude will rub off on you and yours on them.

Life Principle:

Anything that is easy and quick to get will probably have little or no value in life.

> Enter through the narrow gate. For wide is the gate and broad is the road that leads to destruction, and many enter through it. But small is the gate and narrow the road that leads to life, and only a few find it. (Matthew 7:13–14)

Life Principle:

I am whatever the Bible says I am!

There are always different voices around you, voices coming from different sources such as your circumstances and other people, telling you who you are. For example, if you fail an exam, that circumstance may say to you, "If you were a daughter of God, you wouldn't have failed this exam." But the Word of God says, "See what great love the Father has lavished on us, that we should be called children of God! And that is what we are! The reason the world does not know us is that it did not know him" (1 John 3:1).

Do you see the difference between these two voices? The first voice is telling you to see your identity through your circumstances, but the other voice, the voice of God, tells you to hold on to your real and true identity regardless of your situation because your true identity, the one you have in Christ, never changes. The only voice you want to give your ears, heart, soul, and mind to is the Word of God because the Word of God is the only voice that can tell you the real truth about you. You are whatever the Bible says you are!

Life Principle:

No individual is without a problem or imperfection or struggle!

The life stressors and storms we discussed, along with others which are not mentioned in this book, might be the sole reasons a girl chooses to live a sexually impure lifestyle. When we are struggling with serious problems, it can be dangerous to leave them undealt with. Many bad life choices are made by people who are seeking a solution to problems like low self-esteem, peer pressure, fear of rejection or being left alone, or being a victim of sexual abuse. So if you or someone you know is facing any one of these problems, or other, similar ones, you should communicate that with your parents, guardians, or church pastors so that you may get help.

Assignment:

The assignments given in this book can be done individually or together with your CG-STAT group.

1. How do you recognize and avoid a group of friends that may spoil what is good in you? Write down your thoughts or communicate them with your CG-STAT group.
2. If you found a girl who was cutting her arms, how would you help her? Discuss with your group or with your parents.
3. What do you think is the best first step to take if you are experiencing the storms described in this chapter?
4. Where do you look to find an answer for who you are and why you were created?

5. Write a short letter (two to three paragraphs) to yourself, promising yourself that you will study the Word of God to find who you really are and why you are here in this life.

༄

CHAPTER SIX

Male and Female Sexuality

Let me share with you a funny story I heard a long time ago.

After God created the earth, the sun, the moon, the stars, all different animals, and everything else, he decided to create a human being in his own likeness and image. So God made Adam out of the dust of the ground.

He looked at Adam and said, "I can do better than that," and he made Eve.

Well, that might be a funny story, but when we read the Bible, we learn that we are all created by God equally. Even if Eve was taken out of Adam, she too was made out of dust because Adam was made from dust. God made them from dust and breathed life into them. The Bible says:

So God created mankind in his own image,
    in the image of God he created them;
    male and female he created them. (Genesis 1:27)

God created humankind as both man and woman and in his own image. That means both men and women are a reflection of the image of God. They are equal, but they reflect the image of God differently. In essence, they are equally, but differently, created. Why did God create men and women to be different? So that they will complement each other and reflect the *complete* image of God!

Many people today deny the fact that girls and boys are different. Sometimes people even try to tell us that you can choose which you want to be—male or female or something in between. However, as we read in the Bible, God created us male and female—equal and different.

We may find some personality similarities between a male and a female, but although some things may overlap, fundamentally they are different.

These differences are also reflected in the sexuality of male and female. Having a basic understanding of these differences is important. In this chapter, we'll look at how guys' sexuality differs from girls'.

As part of growing up—back to the topic of puberty again!— guys become interested in looking at girls. Instead of admiring the style of clothes or how fashionable she is, guys tend to look at her body parts and shapes.

Guys don't usually dream about chatting with a girl, running in the park with her, or picking flowers together (all of which might be normal dreams for girls). Rather, they dream of the girl's naked body or something similar. Their fantasy typically revolves around the girl's body.

Depending on their exposure to certain movies, magazines, and TV shows, what guys dream about doing with a girl can be unthinkable for girls.

It's important to understand that this isn't wrong all by itself, just like it's not wrong for girls to find themselves attracted to boys and daydreaming about getting married. God has designed male sexuality differently from that of females. Guys are more visually oriented than girls. They get attracted visually. They will especially find themselves staring at a girl who is wearing immodest clothing and exposing her body inappropriately. They can be very quick in sensing the signal a girl is sending to attract them sexually, even if that is not her intention (but often that is the case, consciously or unconsciously). As with girls, natural attraction is not wrong; it's part of God's design. But guys, like girls, can choose what they do with their minds and how they act on what they feel.

Let me summarize the general and basic differences girls and guys have when it comes to sexuality. (Remember that there can be some crossover. Every individual is different. This list is neither comprehensive nor specific to every individual.)

Girls	Guys
Are attracted by what they hear and feel	Are mainly attracted by what they see
Have strong emotional needs	Have strong physical needs, both to see and touch
Desire to bond emotionally, want to share their secrets with a boy they are attracted to	Desire to be physically bonded, want to hold or touch the body of the girl they are attracted to
Seek to talk, hold hands, walk, share their deep secrets as a way of bonding	Seek physical union, the one major way to have deep bonding
Focus on one guy, and everything revolves around him	Can like multiple girls and tend to have compartmentalized thinking—one part of the brain for this girl and the other part for that girl
Flirt with a boy just to play	Flirt with girls to get physical attachment

Tend to be satisfied by attracting a boy or getting his attention	Tend to be satisfied by bonding physically
Physical touch may mean nothing except closeness	Physical touch can trigger the whole cascade of sexual desire to which they tend to want to respond to immediately

Remember, these differences are very important for our lives. Our differences give our lives beauty. Can you imagine if all males thought and acted like females? Yeah, our world wouldn't be a nice place to live in!

These gender differences are something we all need to know about and appreciate so that we won't be misled by ignorance—for example, into thinking that a male thinks about romance and love the same way a girl thinks about those things.

Assignment

The assignments given in this book can be done individually or together with your CG-STAT group.

Okay, we talked about how God is the creator of our sexual desire. With that in mind, do you think God will judge a fourteen-year-old girl with sexual desire who sleeps with a boy? After all, she is far from getting married, and she has this desire in her flesh—a desire she did not create in herself. What do you think about this?

If you are not part of a CG-STAT group, write down your thoughts in your journal, then come back to your answer after you have read the next chapter. If you are part of a CG-STAT group, discuss your thoughts with your group, then return to this question after finishing the next chapter.

⚜

CHAPTER SEVEN

God's Plan and Purpose for Sex

I was giving a five-day seminar about sexuality to teenagers at one local church. Elsa came to the seminar on the last day. I wrapped up with Q&A. She didn't ask any question during the session, but she waited to speak to me personally at the end.

Elsa was sixteen years old when I met her. She had experimented with sex once with one of her classmates. She was still seeing the young man even though her parents didn't approve of her relationship with him. After she told me a little bit about herself and where she was at in life, she said, "I want to ask you one question. Does God care about sex?"

Even if I understood her question, I wanted to know why she was asking. So I asked her, "Why are you asking me that question?"

She replied, "I felt so bad after I had sex with my boyfriend. I know and I think it is sin to have sex before marriage, but why does God care about what I do with my own body?"

Oh, I can't tell you how happy I was that she said that! In her words, I found her real question. And this chapter will go directly into answering Elsa's real question: Why does God care about our bodies?

The Bible says that our body is the temple of the Lord.

> Do you not know that your bodies are temples of the Holy
> Spirit, who is in you, whom you have received from God?
> You are not your own; you were bought at a price. Therefore
> honor God with your bodies. (1 Corinthians 6:19–20)

Imagine! God bought your body at a price, and that price is
the blood of his son, Jesus Christ. And God decided to give what
he bought back to you. Your body is a gift from God. You are to
keep it holy and healthy since it is the temple of the Lord. This gift
is only to be given to one man, your future husband, and that is
done only in matrimony—in marriage. The same is also true for
your husband. He is to keep himself for you alone.

> The wife does not have authority over her own body but
> yields it to her husband. In the same way, the husband does
> not have authority over his own body but yields it to his wife.
> (1 Corinthians 7:4)

We began this book by saying that God has a purpose and plan
for sex. It's time now to discover more about what that plan is.

At this point in your life, you may just be getting interested
in boys, or you may already be dating. It's likely that you will go
through this "searching" phase for years to come. After you go
through the process of meeting different men, you may find one
man who is worthy enough to be your husband. So you two decide
to get married.

After marriage, the Bible says that you two will become one:

> That is why a man leaves his father and mother and is united to
> his wife, and they become one flesh. (Genesis 2:24)

The one and only way the two (one man and one woman) become one is through sexual intercourse and everything else that leads up to their sexual union, including kissing, caressing, and touching.

What Is Sexual Intercourse?

Sexual intercourse is a holy activity, created by God, that is done between a husband and a wife. It's what most people mean when they talk about "having sex." It is the union of a man and a woman through their sexual organs.

If the bride has never slept with anyone, she is called a virgin. Her first sexual experience will be on the first night of her honeymoon. God made an opening for her husband's sexual organ to go in, but that opening is closed by a piece of flesh known as the hymen. On the night of her honeymoon, when her husband's sexual organ enters through her sexual organ, the hymen breaks and she bleeds. For a few days to months after that, she may have pain during sex, but the pain will disappear as she gets used to having intercourse with her husband.

The couple will be one from that time on. The blood is the sign of the covenant made between them and God for both of them to stay together until death parts them.

Sex is the only human activity where two people become one. This oneness is a lasting reality, and according to the Bible, this union should last till death.

Therefore what God has joined together, let no one separate. (Mark 10:9)

At this point you may ask, "Why did God create sex?" Why is it good for man and woman to become one?

The main purposes of sexual intercourse are known as the three Ps:

1. Propagation. It is a commandment of God for his people to make babies so that the earth will be filled with people who are created in his image. (To "propagate" means to continue or increase something. It's often used to mean having children.)

God blessed them and said to them, *"Be fruitful and increase in number*; fill the earth and subdue it. Rule over the fish in the sea and the birds in the sky and over every living creature that moves on the ground." (Genesis 1:28)

2. Protection. God, the creator of our sexual desires, designed a place for our sexual desires to be fulfilled and met, and that is in marriage. When you marry, your sexual desires will be met. If you stay single, you will be vulnerable to temptation to sin sexually. So marriage protects you from falling into sexual sins. (That doesn't mean that all singles are destined to sin sexually or that all married people are immune from sexual temptation and sin. If we don't train ourselves to lead a sexually pure life as the Bible teaches us, we will find ourselves in sexual sin as single or married people.)

Now to the unmarried and the widows I say: It is good for them to stay unmarried, as I do. But if they cannot control themselves, they should marry, for it is better to marry than to burn with passion. (1 Corinthians 7:8–9)

Remember one thing here: We all know that eating an apple every day may prevent us from having different diseases, but apples have never been used to heal anything. In the same way, marriage is designed to protect us from a sexually immoral lifestyle, but it is not designed to heal us from already existing sexually immoral lifestyles.

Just as it is good to eat apple every day to stay healthy, it is good for you to keep yourself away from a sexually immoral lifestyle as a single as well as a married person.

3. Pleasure. While married couples give birth to babies and are protected from sexual immorality, they also have pleasure in their union through sexual intercourse. God created this pleasure as well. Both a wife and a husband can enjoy it.

"May your fountain be blessed,
  and may you rejoice in the wife of your youth. (Proverbs 5:18)

Sexual intimacy between a husband and a wife has many more benefits spiritually, mentally, and physically, but the one major purpose of sex is this: to bond the couple for life so that they become one flesh.

The oneness bond in sex occurs because of sexual hormones that are secreted and released in both bodies during intercourse. These hormones help the couple bond together. These sexual hormones glue them together so that they can live as husband and wife and as father and mother to their children till death does them part. Isn't that amazing? Yes, it is!

And the Two Shall Become . . . Several?

Sleeping with different people and then seeking a marriage that lasts for the long haul is like trying to use one Band-Aid for a knee blister and then taking it off and using it for a blister on some other body. You see, the Band-Aid was made to stick and bond with one blister. If we try to use one Band-Aid for different blisters, it will lose its adhesiveness and come off easily.

This is very close to the truth about the nature of sex. Just like one Band-Aid is perfectly good for only one blister, God created us so that one woman will bond sexually with only one man. That is mentally, physically, spiritually, and emotionally right for us.

It is very risky to sleep with multiple guys and then marry one of them and try to bond with him. Other than the other mental, spiritual, emotional, and physical consequences for having premarital sex (with one or multiple men), it creates havoc to the future marital sexual relationship.

Some may argue, saying, "Well, I only slept with one guy. So that must be okay." I will say more about this in the next chapter, but let me say this here: When God put sex in marriage, he knew that marriage was not only perfect place for sex to happen but it also a perfect fit for our nature as God created us. Outside God's design, we only end up hurting ourselves in ways we may not recover from.

For a girl who has had sex before marriage and now wants to have a marriage according to the Word of God, it may require counseling, confession of sin, and a change of heart and lifestyle before she will be able to experience sexual fulfillment in marriage as God designed it. After that, the forgiveness of God can renew her life and bring healing to her marriage before her marriage "comes off" like that secondhand Band-Aid.

God is the creator of sex, and he is the one with the right guidelines for sex—not TV, not magazines, not your teacher, not your friends, and not your feelings or emotions.

God knows what is good for you because he is the one who made you. He made you and gave you a user's manual in the Bible to guide you into a fulfilled, abundant, and joyful life.

The thief [the devil] comes only to steal and kill and destroy;
I [Jesus] came that they may have life, and have *it* abun-
dantly. (John 10:10, NASB)

When you choose a lifestyle that is not according to God's
Word but according to the fairy tale created by this world, you are
giving up a God-given healthy, joyful, fulfilled, and abundant life
through Christ Jesus. God's purposes and plans for sex are *beyond*
the fairy tale—they're better, more romantic, and more fulfilling
in the end.

Life Principle:

**God doesn't do anything without plan and purpose and all
his plans and purposes are good, and pleasing for us.**

"For I know the plans I have for you," declares the LORD,
"plans to prosper you and not to harm you, plans to give you
hope and a future." (Jeremiah 29:11)

Assignment

*The assignments given in this book can be done individually or
together with your CG-STAT group.*

Why do you think God gives us a sexual desire way before we
are ready to get married? You can discuss this question with your
parents and write your answer in your book. After you read the
next chapter, come back to your answer and see if there is anything you want to change. If you are part of the CG-STAT, discuss
it with your group.

CHAPTER EIGHT

✤

Why Wait to Have Sex Until Marriage?

Mike, who was twenty years old, and Danielle, who was seventeen, had been seeing each other for two months. On their last date, driving her around a small neighborhood, Mike asked Danielle to sleep with him. That was not the first time he'd asked, but it was when he came through to her with full force. Inside her heart she wanted to say "No," but he had some convincing points.

"We are both Christians, and sex is not something bad. It is a good thing. God is the one who gave us sex to enjoy. Sex becomes bad only when we do it with multiple people. Both of us have never had sex with anyone before, and we love each other and nothing can separate us. Sex is something that will help us to be together forever. What kind of God would give us sexual desire and tell us to wait? Is that the God you are worshiping?"

Even though it's been a year since Danielle gave in to Mike's talk and lost her virginity, the whole thing feels for her like it happened yesterday. As a seventeen-year-old girl, she had already dreamt about marrying Mike and having kids and living happily ever after.

When I met Danielle, she was struggling with one particular

question: Why does God give us sexual desire way before we are ready for marriage?

It feels unfair for God to expect us to wait to have sex until marriage. That's a fair reasoning. Isn't it?

If a small child asks his parents to cook, they won't say, "Okay, go ahead and cook," knowing the danger of an oven or stove. A child has to first grow up enough to learn how and when to use kitchen appliances appropriately.

Let's say you decide to be part of your state's marathon race. You go to your state's YWCA (Young Women's Christian Association) and register. If they call you the next day to run for a marathon race, what will be your reaction?

Do you say, "No, I can't run"? After all, you *can* run. You have everything you need to run. You have two legs. You have a pair of eyes to see where you're going. You have a brain to understand where and when to start and stop the race. You also have a desire to run. What else do you need?

Well, there is one thing missing. What do you think it is? It is called COMPETENCY. You must have the mental and physical competency necessary before you can safely take part in a marathon.

Marathon runners go through rigorous training which develops in them not only physical strength for the actual race, but dedication and self-control.

While you are young and single, you prepare for sex not by doing it, but by getting mature enough mentally, physically, emotionally, and spiritually to handle every responsibility that comes with sexual intercourse.

During singleness, you mature mentally, physically, emotionally, and spiritually to become that girl who will be a good wife to her husband and a responsible mother to her children.

Sexual temptations and other temptations are not there to destroy you but to make you a better person. Through it all, you can learn how to walk closer to God, depend on him completely, and lead a victorious life in him. You can learn patience as you wait for the right time for you to find your Prince Charming. You can learn how to trust God as you trust him to help you see and meet that man who is going to be your beloved husband for life. You will learn to respect yourself and others. You will also get the most important life skill there is, one that many young people don't have—self-control. With self-control, you can direct your life path according to the Word of God, not according to your wrong desires or your friends' desires. You will train yourself to say no to things that are not legitimately yours. You will learn how to be the boss of your body and desires, not the other way around.

There is no one couple who is a perfect match, and there is no one marriage where conflicts and disagreements can't be found. Even after doing everything right, following every recommended biblical step, married couples still face struggles in their marriage. Why? Because, for the perfect marriage to happen, two perfect people have to get married and none of us are perfect! The other reason is that oneness is a process, not a one-night deal, and it is a process both husband and wife are involved in, actively working toward the goal of complete oneness. Sexual purity now is an important part of preparing for that process!

Just because couples are married, it doesn't mean they won't struggle. Life is full of ups and downs. During your time of singleness, you will learn how to handle different situations before you handle difficult ones you find in the marriage. Singleness is a time for you to learn how to walk in holiness. Some people expect marriage to cleanse them from sinful lifestyles. That is a big misconception. Marriage protects people from sexual immorality, but it is not designed to heal anybody from sexually immoral lifestyles.

> How can a young person stay on the path of purity?
>   By living according to your word. (Psalm 119:9)

> I have hidden your word in my heart
>   that I might not sin against you. (Psalm 119:11)

The other thing you should remember is this: Just because a person is married doesn't mean that she won't face sexual temptation. All married people face sexual temptation in one way or the other.

The difference is this: If you strengthen your "sexual purity muscle" while you are single, the chance for you to stumble in sexual sin while you're married will be much slimmer, assuming that after marriage you continue abiding in the Word of God.

The authors of *Every Young Woman's Battle,* Shannon Ethridge and Stephen Arterburn, give this example about the danger of having sex outside marriage:

> Fire allows us to heat our homes, cook our food, and sterilize instruments. It also provides us with a great amount of enjoyment as we snuggle around a warm fireplace on a cold winter evening.
>
> But despite fire's many benefits, it can also be very dangerous—just ask the hundreds of people who lost their homes to the fires that raged out of control for weeks in Southern California . . . Failing to understand or respect the destructive potential of fire can cause great pain rather than pleasure . . . When used

properly within the boundaries God established for sex—only within marriage—a woman's sexual desires draw her toward her husband for a deeper level of emotional connection and physical pleasure than she can find in any other earthly relationship.

Sexual purity is foundational to the rest of your life. Let's say your parents decide to buy a house, and they go to see one that is on sale. While the real estate agent is giving them a tour, he says this: "You guys are very lucky to have this house. It is made from the most expensive material there is. It has five bedrooms and five full bathrooms. And it was built just five years ago. The only one problem is that every night, there is an earthquake that shakes the house from its foundation. But that's all—everything else is great!"

What would your parents' reaction be? They might think the man has lost his mind for expecting them to buy a house that doesn't even have a firm foundation. It doesn't matter how good the house may look, if it doesn't have a foundation that can hold the house in place, it is useless—and it is dangerous.

Just like that, not having self-disciple and self-control in the sexual area of your life brings a serious problem in the other areas of your life as well.

Better a patient person than a warrior,
   one with self-control than one who takes a city.
   (Proverbs 16:32)

As you train yourself to have self-discipline and control in your sexual life, you learn to yield your desires and dreams to God, and you can find out how faithful God is in meeting your desires and needs and bringing your dreams into reality. Yes, God rewards your effort.

Singleness, rather than a time to experiment sexually and have multiple boyfriends and partners, is a time for you to prayerfully look for a man to live your life with until death parts you. You see, life is not as it is portrayed in Hollywood movies. The fairy tale of meeting someone, falling instantly and madly in love, and kissing in the moonlight is far from the real picture. Finding a life partner, a husband, takes time, energy, and lots of advice from different people, and it requires mental, physical, emotional, and spiritual maturity.

In all your ways acknowledge Him,
And He will make your paths straight. (Proverbs 3:6)

Animals are given over to their instincts, desires, feelings, and wants, to be totally controlled by them. That is not true of you, the daughter of God!

When a dog senses sexual desire, he follows that desire until he fulfills it. But you who are created in the image of God don't lead your life by your instincts but by the spirit of God and by the truths found in the Bible, the Word of God.

When a girl is given over to desires, emotions, and feelings, and disregards God and his words, she ends up in a life that is not part of her dreams. Who would dream of being miserable and broken in every area of life? No one!

Those who live according to the flesh have their minds set on what the flesh desires; but those who live in accordance with the Spirit [the Spirit of God or the Word of God] have their minds set on what the Spirit desires. The mind governed by the flesh is death, but the mind governed by the Spirit is life and peace. The mind governed by the flesh is hostile to God; it does not submit to God's law, nor can it do so. Those who are in the realm of the flesh cannot please God. (Romans 8:5–8)

Many relationships fail from the beginning because they start with sex. Sex was created and designed by God, and God is the only one who knows the right time for sex to happen.

According to the Bible, the only right place for sex is within marriage.

Marriage should be honored by all, and the marriage bed kept pure, for God will judge the adulterer and all the sexually immoral. (Hebrews 13:4)

In God's plan, sexual union comes as the last step after commitment (promising to live together till the end), covenant (exchanging vows before God and others), and oneness in other areas of life, such as emotionally, spiritually, and mentally. When a couple knows that they are able to live together and raise a family, they exchange wedding vows before God and others. They may not have an expensive wedding with two thousand invited guests or a big house to live in. All they need is guests from each side, a pastor, and God, all of whom act as witnesses of their vows, and a marriage certificate so the government of the land they live in will legally recognize the marriage. After they exchange their vows, they are called husband and wife, and they finish the process of bonding for life by sleeping together, starting from the honeymoon night.

Why is it important for sex to come last in a relationship? Well, have you ever solved a puzzle where you have to keep one piece on the side because you know for sure it comes at the end and if you put it first, it will get very hard to get the rest of the puzzle into place? Or have you ever set up a Christmas tree?

At what point do you put that twinkling star on the Christmas tree? You put it on after you finish putting all the ornaments and the lights! It's the final, celebratory moment that finishes all the rest.

Well, sexual intercourse is just like that. It should be the last step that occurs after couples become one in all other areas of life.

Remember that quote from *Every Young Woman's Battle*? The authors compare fire in a fireplace to a wildfire in the forest. Both are fire, but they have two major differences. One has a boundary and the other one doesn't have a boundary; one is controlled by a man, and the other one controls men. No one can tell a wildfire to go "this far" or "that far," and no one can predict the damage it will cause. On the other hand, a fireplace fire has a boundary. It is limited to burning as long as it's permitted to by the owner of the fireplace, and it is there to benefit the family of that house. The family, not the fire itself, decides when to turn the flames on or off.

When sex is placed in its rightful place, it is like a fire in a fireplace. It benefits the man and the woman, the whole household, and the society at large. Think about it: If everybody decides to faithfully have sex only in marriage, there won't be a chance to commit adultery or fornication; no children will be born out of wedlock; nobody gets hurt.

When sex is practiced outside marriage, it is like a raging wildfire—it destroys life, and the hurt it may bring cannot be predicted. It won't have any boundaries to limit its consequences. Nobody knows where or when the hurt and damage it brings to life will stop, and no one can predict the extent of the damage it is going to cause.

Just as wildfires in Southern California and other western states can cause property and human casualties, sex outside marriage may be the cause of dysfunction in families, hurt, sickness, abortion (the killing of the baby in the mother's womb), divorce, and even death for some people.

Sacred Sex

Sexual intercourse between a married couple can be a very sacred and spiritual activity. This is also part of God's design. Sexual intercourse has at least two amazing spiritual implications which we need to pay attention to.

Genesis 1 and 2 are the story of creation—chapter 1 is the summary and chapter 2 is the detail. As you probably remember, God created Adam out of dust and breathed life into him. Then God took Eve out of Adam so that Adam wouldn't be alone. You see, Eve was created at the same time as Adam; it's just that she was part of the body of Adam originally.

Genesis 2:23–24 reads like this:

The man said,
"This is now bone of my bones
and flesh of my flesh;
she shall be called 'woman,'
for she was taken out of man."
That is why a man leaves his father and mother and is united
to his wife, and they become one flesh.

Adam and Eve originally were one; both of them existed in one body. Then God took Eve out of Adam, and they became two. I heard one Bible teacher say something like this: "God took

Eve out of Adam, and they both have a desire to be back to their original place. They have 'the urge to merge.' That urge to merge is the sexual desire both male and female have."

Through sexual intercourse, the man and woman "become one flesh." Through sex, they return back to the original "Adam," the man who has Eve in him; the one who was created in God's own image. *That* is the complete picture of the image of God.

Can you just imagine the joy and pleasure of God when he sees the original Adam he created?

But wait! There is another amazing truth to sexual intercourse also. When you read Ephesians 5 verses 22 through 33, you will find instruction as to how a wife and a husband should behave in a marriage. A wife is instructed to submit to her husband like the church submits to Christ, and a husband is instructed to love his wife as Christ loved the Church and gave himself up for her. In Revelation, the writer describes an amazing event: the wedding of the Lamb (Christ) with his Bride, the Church. It depicts the picture of Christ's oneness with his Bride.

You see, when a man marries a woman according to the Word of God, and when the two become one flesh through sex, they reflect the picture of the original Adam back to God through their oneness, and their oneness also foretells the oneness of Christ and his Bride, the Church, the oneness we all are waiting for that will happen at the end of this world.

Do you see how God loves sexual intercourse but how the devil hates it? The devil tries everything to deceive us in this area so that the complete and one-flesh image of Adam won't reflect the image of God, *and* so that the coming of Christ and his oneness with his Church will not be proclaimed through sexual intercourse.

It is good for all of us to do the will of God in every part of our lives, because that is the only way we can get the abundant life God has promised to us. It is not good to have sex before marriage because it is not the best for us; it will destroy us. Our nature is suited perfectly to the will of God because he created us in his way for his will to go well with us.

So save sex for the night of your honeymoon! You will never regret it!

Life Principle:
"If you play with fire, you will get burned."

It is a very easy concept for all of us to grasp that it's dangerous to touch fire. We all learned at an early age that we can't just touch fire and go without getting burned. Sex is like fire when we try to have it outside marriage. We will get "burned," or hurt by regret, guilt, despair, depression, and so on. That is why the Bible compares having sex outside the boundary of marriage with hot coals on our body. Listen:

> Can a man scoop fire into his lap
>   without his clothes being burned?
> Can a man walk on hot coals
>   without his feet being scorched?
> So is he who sleeps with another man's wife;
>   no one who touches her will go unpunished. (Proverbs 6:27–29)

Assignment
The assignments given in this book can be done individually or together with your CG-STAT group.

Let's say an eighteen-year-old girl, let's call her Esther, decides to date an eighteen-year-old guy. After their fourth date, the guy says to her, "Okay, I love you more than I ever expected myself to be in love with a girl. I don't think I will ever have a desire to look for another girl. I want to marry you and have a family together. Since we're not going to be apart, it is okay to start to have sex now. What do you say?"

How would you advise this girl to respond to him if she came to you for advice? Write down your answer. If you are in a CG-STAT group, share your answers and talk about the reasons for the advice you would give.

CHAPTER NINE

Fight for the Sexual Pleasure God Destined You to Have

After being in slavery for four hundred years, the Israelites cried out to God to save them. So God sent Moses to lead the people out of slavery, out of Egypt, and to bring them to the Promised Land, saying, "So I have come down to rescue them from the hand of the Egyptians and to bring them up out of that land into a good and spacious land, a land flowing with milk and honey" (Exodus 3:8).

With his brother, Aaron, Moses came to the elders of the Israelites and told them what God had said. (You can read the story of the Israelites journey from Egypt to the Promised Land in the Bible, starting with the book of Exodus and reading to the book of Joshua).

You can just imagine how excited the people were to be free from slavery and to live on the land that flowed milk and honey! But the one thing the Israelites didn't know was that they were supposed to wage war against the wilderness and the people who were living on the Promised Land at the time. God had already promised to them that the Promised Land belonged to them, but they didn't realize that they were actually supposed to engage in an actual war to get to it. God not only promised them the land, but he also promised them that he would be with them and fight for them (Exodus 23:27).

God didn't say to them, "Just watch TV while you eat chips and live as you like while I take you to the Promised Land." No, he didn't say that. Even though he promised them the Land and that his presence would be with them all the way (Exodus 13:21–22), he told them to obey him and his commands and to engage in the war for the long haul.

Just as God was for the Israelites, he is for you. He fights for you. He is on your side, and he has your best interests at heart.

As we have seen, God created sex by plan and purpose. He knows what sex is. God is not ashamed of sex or any of the actions involved with it.

But the devil, knowing that sex is a precious gift of God for humans, has been in the business of destroying its true meaning and purpose in the lives of people for a long time! Since sex is a powerful tool, he has been using it like a wildfire to bring hurt and destruction—and so far, he's been fairly successful in his plan.

One of the consequences of sex outside of God's plan is that it will put you far from the pleasure and fulfillment of sexual intimacy which is legitimately yours. If you get married, you are destined for sexual pleasure in God's plan. The devil would like to destroy that, but you can fight for it!

Fighting the Lies

As the Bible says in John 8:44, the devil is the father of lies. He lies and deceives us at every opportunity. He will use anything to get his lies into our heart so that we believe them as truth.

Today, the entertainment business is one of the main avenues the devil uses to spread his lies. In most movies, TV shows, and soap operas today—not to mention music, books, and magazines!— he prescribes sex for everyone, including those who are as young as sixteen or even younger. He lies to us, encouraging us to get that fire burning. He says there will be no consequences; that sex outside of marriage is exciting, fun, and harmless.

The devil has always been a liar! He even tried to deceive Jesus. Notice how Jesus, the Son of God, defeated the devil in the book of Matthew, chapter 4. For each deceiving statement the devil threw at Jesus, Jesus replied by saying "It is written . . ." That means he quoted the Bible back at the devil. He fought the devil's lies with the truths of God's Word.

Remember, the devil is a spirit. That means he fights with you in spirit, and you need to fight him back in spirit.

> For our struggle is not against flesh and blood, but against the rulers, against the authorities, against the powers of this dark world and against the spiritual forces of evil in the heavenly realms. (Ephesians 6:12)

So how do you fight with the dark spiritual forces?

> For though we live in the world, we do not wage war as the world does. The weapons we fight with are not the weapons of the world. On the contrary, they have divine power to demolish strongholds. We demolish arguments and every pretension that sets itself up against the knowledge of God, and we take captive every thought to make it obedient to Christ. (2 Corinthians 10:5)

Your weapon against these spiritual forces of evil is the Word of God. Just like Jesus, you need to be fully armored with the Word of God, which is the only armor and weapon you have. You, the child of God, need to wear the full armor of God at all times:

> Therefore put on the full armor of God, so that when the day of evil comes, you may be able to stand your ground, and after you have done everything, to stand. Stand firm then, with *the belt of truth* buckled around your waist, with *the breast-plate of righteousness* in place, and with your feet fitted with the readiness that comes from *the gospel of peace*. In addition to all this, take up *the shield of faith*, with which you can extinguish all the flaming arrows of the evil one. Take the helmet of salvation and the sword of the Spirit, which is *the Word of God*. And *pray in the Spirit* on all occasions with all kinds of prayers and requests. With this in mind, be alert and always keep on praying for all the saints. (Ephesians 6:13–18, emphasis added)

Notice something here: The Word of God is the only weapon you have to attack your enemy. The other pieces of armor are there to protect you.

So how do you get into this armor? When you read, study, and meditate on the Word of God daily, and then you do your best to live out what you are reading, it creates in you all of these pieces of armor. Let me give you one example: The Bible says that faith comes from hearing the Word of God (Romans 10:17). As you read, study, and meditate (which can include saying the verse repeatedly), your heart and mind will hear the Word. And faith comes to your heart because of that process. As you do this, you will also find it easier to obey the Word. Do you see how the Word of God is foundational for your walk as a Christian? For you to have all the armor, the Word of God is the first and most basic thing you need to focus on.

When you are armed with the Word of God, you can fight like Jesus. When a thought that is against the Word of God—a lie—comes to your mind, you need to fight it back with the Word of God that opposes the lie.

Let me give you some practical examples to show you how you can use the Word of God to win the war that is waging inside you:

Devil's Lie: "Be sexy, flirt with boys. Otherwise you will be all alone forever."

That is a pure lie! You may not remember an exact Bible verse, but if you train yourself up in studying the Bible and meditating on its verses during your quiet time with the Lord, you will easily remember words that can attack this particular thought without remembering the exact chapter and verse. You're not alone in this. Reminding us of the truth of God in times of need is one of the most important works of the Holy Spirit in our lives. It's not important to remember the exact chapter and verse numbers. What matters is that you know the words of God.

So when a lie comes to you, take out a verse from your memory bank and say it back to the devil as Jesus did. You may only need one, as long as it is one that directly opposes the thought.

So for the devil's lie that says,*"Be sexy, flirt with boys. Otherwise you will be all alone forever"*, a weapon to use is:

It is written:

"The LORD is my shepherd, I shall not be in want." (Psalm 23:1)

Or "I will never leave you nor forsake you." (Joshua 1:5)

Or "No one who hopes in you will ever be put to shame." (Psalm 25:3)

Or "The lions may grow weak and hungry, but those who seek the Lord lack no good thing" (Psalm 34:10).

Devil's Lie: "You fell for this sin last week. Why do you try not to do it again? It is impossible for you to stop."

A weapon to use is:

It is written:

"I can do all things through Him [Christ] who strengthens me." (Philippians 4:13, NASB)

Or "My help comes from the Lord, the Maker of heaven and earth." (Psalm 121:2)

Or "What is impossible with man is possible with God." (Luke 18:27)

Or "The one who is in you is greater than the one who is in the world." (1 John 4:4)

(You can personalize Bible verses such as these by saying them this way: "The One who is in me is greater than the one who is in the world.")

Devil's Lie: "You don't need to go to church or pray and read the Bible with others. You don't need anybody's help. That is for the weak people. You can do it yourself. You have strong willpower."

A weapon to use is:

It is written:

"How good and pleasant it is when God's people live together in unity! . . . For there the Lord bestows his blessing, even life forevermore." (Psalm 133:1–3)

Satan knows that God has ordained blessing and life which is only found in the fellowship of brothers and sisters in Christ. And he wants to keep you from that life and blessing so that he can influence you with his values and messages, which lead to death.

Truth-and-Lie Soup

There is one other thing I want you to remember here: Satan doesn't always come to you with a 100 percent lie. He often comes with 99 percent truth but 1 percent lie. That 1 percent lie can throw you off track if you believe it as truth. The devil likes to mix truth and lies into a soup to make it harder for you to tell the difference. But the Word of God can still give you the insight and wisdom to help you recognize the whole truth!

Let's see some examples.

Devil's Lie: "God never blames anyone for enjoying life."

Yes, it is true that God doesn't blame anyone for enjoying life. In fact, he wants us to enjoy our lives! But God doesn't want his children getting hurt in the name of enjoying life.

God gets hurt when you destroy your tomorrows by your present poor choices. When God tells you to do or not to do something, and you choose to disobey him, your choice will ultimately hurt you really badly. If God says, "This is not good for you," it will never be good for you in any situation or circumstance. God doesn't lie or compromise. He is the One who created you, and he is the only One who knows what is best for you.

You cannot disobey God and enjoy life at the same time.

So the weapon you need to use is something like this:

It is written:

"Be sure of this: The wicked will not go unpunished,
   but those who are righteous will go free." (Proverbs 11:21)

Or "'There is no peace,' says my God, 'for the wicked.'" (Isaiah 57:21)

Devil's Lie: "You are too far away from God's mercy and grace."

There is no sin that Christ's blood can't cleanse. If you sin against God, you can come back to him and confess your sin. He is just and faithful to forgive you and enable you to get back on track. You see, God forgives everyone who comes to him. You will never be beyond the reach of God's forgiving grace as long as there is breath in your lungs.

A weapon to use is:

It is written:

"If we confess our sins, he is faithful and just and will forgive us our sins and purify us from all unrighteousness." (1 John 1:9)

Or "The thief [the devil] comes only to steal and kill and destroy; *I [Jesus] have come that they may have life, and have it to the full.*" (John 10:10, emphasis added)

Devil's Lie: "After all, God is a forgiving God, and he will forgive you as he forgave all the people who've done this sin."

Yes, it is true that God forgives everyone who comes to him, but forgiveness does not free anyone from the consequences of sin. That means the quicker and the sooner you confess your sins and change your course of life to conform to the life God desires for you to have, the less the consequences of sin you may have to endure. When you can enjoy life to the fullest *today*, why do you want to postpone it?

A weapon to use:

It is written:

"I tell you, now is the time of God's favor, now is the day of salvation." (2 Corinthians 6:2)

Devil's Lie: "Everybody is different, and you are unique. Your situation is different from others. So don't blame yourself for doing this."

Yes, it is true that everybody is different and unique, but when it comes to sexual purity or immorality—or any sin—every follower of Christ Jesus is called to lead a holy and pure life. There is no partiality with God, and there is no other alternative life than a holy and pure life before God through Christ!

Weapons to use:

It is written:

"Be holy, because I am holy." (1 Peter 1:16, Leviticus 11:44–45)

Or "For God did not call us to be impure, but to live a holy life" (1 Thessalonians 4:7)

The Facts of Life

Knowing some important life facts can also help you defeat and ignore the devil's lies. The devil loves for us to be ignorant! Let's see some examples:

Devil's Lie: "Men love girls who are easy."

They do if they are looking for "a toy" to play with! Not all men are the same, and not all men are looking for a toy. Don't forget this: Good men are around, and they are looking for a girl to love, respect, cherish, and treasure. There may not be many of them, but they are around.

Devil's Lie: "Everybody is having sex."

Although many people around you are having sex, there are millions of people who are not. There are millions of girls and guys out there who are waiting on God and for marriage before they will have sex.

Do you remember the story of Samuel? He grew up in a place where everybody, including the sons of Eli, the high priest, used to sleep around. Samuel did not take part in their sinful lifestyles, and God rewarded him in everything he did. (Read the first and second books of Samuel to learn more about his story.)

Devil's Lie: "Your parents don't know anything about your life because they are from a different generation" or *"Keep this secret from your parents. After all, they won't understand you or what you're going through because they are from a different culture and generation."*

We already saw that your parents are on your side. If your parents are busy or are not available to talk to you or if you feel that your parents don't understand you at all, it is wise for you to find a mentor in your church—and older woman who can counsel you and give you guidance.

Life Principle:
The root of all kinds of destructive lifestyles get conceived first in the mind.

If you ever have to wage war to bring change to your life, you have to start from your mind because that is where the root is—that is where the change needs to begin to bring a lasting and permanent change to your life. That means the best way to protect yourself and your life from adopting destructive lifestyles and habits is by fighting for your mind, guarding it from any thoughts which can become action tomorrow and make your life difficult.

Listen what the Bible says where our sinful thoughts and desires lead us into:

> When tempted, no one should say, "God is tempting me." For God cannot be tempted by evil, nor does he tempt anyone; but each person is tempted when they are dragged away by their own evil desire and enticed. Then, after desire has conceived, it gives birth to sin; and sin, when it is full-grown, gives birth to death. (James 1:13–15)

Assignment:

The assignments given in this book can be done individually or together with your CG-STAT group.

How do you fight the following devil's lie with the Word of God: "You are not as beautiful as Selena Gomez."

Discuss this with your parents or older siblings and write down as many Bible verses as you can think of to fight back this lie. If you are part of CG-STAT, discuss your answer with your group.

*

CHAPTER TEN

Battling for Your Mind

The one thing in the technological world that is close to how our brain works is a computer. Of course, our brain is much, much more complicated than our laptops, but for the sake of making a point, let's assume that our laptops are like our brain or thought center—our mind.

If we view our brain cells and muscles as all the wiring of our laptops, we can view all the thoughts we take in from different sources as the important software we download.

You and I know that there are notorious software viruses out there, viruses which can turn all our files into nothing within a second. So we need to have some sort of antivirus protection to protect our laptops and all our files and the software we have downloaded.

In the same way, we need to have the Word of God as our antivirus, downloaded into our minds. Without the Word of God being "downloaded" in our minds, our insight about life, including the message of sexual purity, will be messed up and tend to be conformed to the insight of this world's "viruses" or ways of thinking.

Just like computer hackers don't attack the CEOs of big companies but go after their computer systems, the devil always attacks your mind first. He tries to win your mind by sending to your thoughts his "viruses"— his thoughts and lies that are against the Word and will of God.

The devil wants to win your thought life because he knows that once he wins your thought life, the rest will be as easy as saying "one, two, three."

For as he thinketh in his heart, so is he. (Proverbs 23:7, KJV)

If you dwell on the thought of having sex or getting involved in a sinful act, you will soon act it out. It is just a matter of time. But if you dwell in the Word of God, the Word of God itself will fight back any thought that comes against it.

Knowing the Word of God, living and abiding in God's Word, and knowing how to use it when you face the devil's lies will benefit you throughout your life.

Do not merely listen to the word, and so deceive yourselves. Do what it says. (James 1:22)

Doing and obeying the Word of God makes the truth of God part of who you are. The Word of God that is planted in your heart is like a seed. You need to protect and nourish it for it to flourish in your life. One way for you to protect "the seed" of the Word is by staying away from those things which may corrupt the truth of God that is planted in your heart.

What do I mean by that? Let's say you stay in the Word for a week and then go to a movie theater and watch one R-rated movie that has no moral values. You will come out of there spiritually empty, just as if you didn't have the Word of God in your heart. Why? Because those things you watch will steal the precious truth of God from your heart, and you won't have any spiritual power to fight back against the devil and his lies. Not only that, but what you are watching will also make your heart resistant to hearing and obeying the Word of God. (On your own time, read the parable of the sower found in Matthew 13:1–23. These are important truths!)

However, even after knowing and doing all the things you know to be biblically true and right, you may stumble and fall. If you do, you have to come back to the throne of God, ask forgiveness, and start all over again.

As physical and mental maturity come through a process, so does spiritual maturity. You may fall, but you decide to come back again through confession and repentance, to change and forsake your sinful ways. As you remain in God and his Word, little by little you will lose interest in being part of anything that is offensive to the Lord. Little by little, you start having a strong desire to make your heavenly Father happy, and you start realizing how beneficial God and his words are to your life.

Strategies to Escape the Trap of Satan

In order to stay out of the trap of the enemy, you need life strategies.

You can pray and talk to wise leaders about what other strategies to use, but your life strategies should at least include the following things:

1. Listen to, respect, and honor your parents.

    Although I said much about this topic in the second chapter, it won't hurt to say it again: Honoring and respecting your parents and obeying them brings glory and praise to God and many blessings to your life. It will make your life, as the Bible says, "go well." Since God is the one who chose them to be parents to you, when you respect and honor them, you are respecting and honoring God who gave them to you and commanded you to respect and honor them. And guess what? Sometimes, even many times, your parents can see danger coming. They may tell you to do or not to do something. When you obey them (even if it doesn't make sense to you), you are saving your life from lots of hurts and pains because God rewards obedience.

Children, obey your parents in the Lord, for this is right . . . you know that the Lord will reward each one for whatever good they do. (Ephesians 6:1, 8)

2. Have your own private prayer time every day.

Most spiritual leaders highly recommend having a prayer time when you are mostly awake and energetic. You may skip this day and that day, but still, having a set time to be with the Lord is a very important Christian discipline to develop. You will mature spiritually and emotionally as you get older and grow into womanhood.

3. Read the Bible every day, meditate on the Word day and night, and strive to apply the Word in your life with the help of God.

Remember, life won't crumble in a day. It takes time to build or demolish it. If you establish a private devotional time, which includes prayer and Bible reading time, and you spend time fellowshipping with other Christians, you can correct any wrong path from the start. God will speak to you through his Word and other people or situations.

Don't try to live a pure life depending on your own

willpower or anything other than the help of the Holy Spirit. Just like the people of Israel needed manna from the sky on a daily basis (Exodus 16), and just like you need to eat and drink daily to live physically, you also need to study, meditate, and live on the Word of God daily so that you can live, grow, and mature spiritually. As manna was for the Israelite people to eat and be physically healthy, so the Word of God is for you to live a spiritually healthy life. When you mature spiritually and mentally, you can see the trap of the devil from far away and spare your life many troubles.

Man does not live on bread alone but on every word that comes from the mouth of the LORD. (Deuteronomy 8:3)

The Word itself cleanses you and your life.

How can a young person stay on the path of purity? By living according to your word. (Psalm 119:9)

The Word itself prevents you from sinning against God.

I have hidden your word in my heart that I might not sin against you. (Psalm 119:11)

The Word itself leads you on the right path, the path that is acceptable and pleasing to God and that doesn't include the trap of the enemy.

Your word is a lamp for my feet, a light on my path. (Psalm 119:105)

Remember, the Word of God is the only weapon you have against your enemy. Using it will protect you from making harmful life choices.

4. Be friends with other believers who have the same moral values and convictions as you do.

   Don't be "unequally yoked" with those who don't have the same beliefs and convictions as you do (2 Corinthians 6:14). That is a dangerous trap of the enemy! Find two or three girls who can be your accountability partners and with whom you can talk about anything. They can ask you how you're doing in your walk with Jesus, and you can ask them the same. They pray for you, you pray for them; they advise you when you need it and you do the same; they tell you when you are drifting away from Christ and you do the same. You can call them at any time and they can call you too; you can tell them your secrets, and they can trust you as well. It is challenging to find that kind of friendship, but if you are that kind of friend already, it will not be too hard to find one like you. Be the first one to start that kind of relationship. Don't wait for one person to open up. Be that person to break the ice. Be that person who keeps other people's secrets as her own and develops trust in the relationship.

Flee the evil desires of youth and pursue righteousness, faith, love and peace, along with those who call on the Lord out of a pure heart. (2 Timothy 2:22)

You can be strong to fight back the pressure that comes from others through finding friends who have similar moral values and convictions like you. You may find friends like that in your church or school. But as a precaution here: Not everybody who goes to church is a Christian. Many people in churches may not even believe in the Bible. They may profess to be Christians, they may have perfect church attendance, and they may even use some Bible verses here and there in their conversation, but they may not be Christians.

The Bible says this regarding these kinds of people:

> But now I am writing to you that you must not associate with anyone who claims to be a brother or sister but is sexually immoral or greedy, an idolater or slanderer, a drunkard or swindler. Do not even eat with such people. (1 Corinthians 5:11)

5. Know the basic nature of men.

Remember, men are not women!

Sex is mainly a physical need for men. Every seventy-two hours, they have what is called a "sperm build-up" in their bodies, and when that happens, they have to get a release. God naturally installed in men a mechanism called "nocturnal emission," also known as a "wet dream." Before marriage, men get release from sperm build-up through this mechanism, releasing the sperm while they are sleeping. But not all men are satisfied with this mechanism. Living in a sexually saturated society, men are exposed to strong and hard-to-resist sexual temptations. When a man finds himself in that situation and yields to temptation, he will go beyond what is permitted for him and do anything to get a girl to sleep with him.

When a guy pursues a girl for sex, he may act as if he is deeply in love with her. She may interpret his sweet words and "I can't sleep without looking at your eyes" text messages as love. Rather, for many men, it just means he is interested in having a sexual relationship with her. When his sexual hormones, which can get out of control if not tamed appropriately, go through the roof, he may say or do anything to convince a girl to sleep with him.

Remember, even well-intentioned men can say and do unthinkable things if they give in to temptation. It's your sole responsibility to protect yourself from being exposed to a bad situation.

Nowadays, most girls don't want to wait until marriage to have sex. It is not because they consciously choose to be sexually promiscuous; rather, they become the product of what they are exposed to. They might be victims of media, peer pressure, or even teachers who tell them to be sexually promiscuous and dress in such a way as to seduce men in order to be considered "cool" or "attractive."

Because most girls in our society accept this lifestyle as a norm, if a girl believes in sexual abstinence, she may face ridicule. Some girls will do anything to escape that ridicule, even to the point of letting go of their virginity and their spiritual convictions. More often than not, most girls who have lost their virginity encourage other girls to do the same. Why? Because *misery loves company!* This means a girl who has lost her virginity may want to hang out with people who are like her. If you are different from her, she may try anything to convince or belittle you until you join her "club."

One young man was ridiculed by his junior varsity team members in the locker room because he was a virgin. One day, he confronted them and said:

"I can be like you guys anytime I want to, but you guys can never be like me, forever."

6. Remember, not every guy who goes to church is a Christian. Even if he looks and sounds like a Christian to you, make sure you don't give in to his "I can't love any other woman but you" statements. Have clear life boundaries.

A *boundary* is a limit or bound. In the case of sexual purity, having boundaries means limiting how close you will let a boy come to you, or how much you will allow him to talk to or touch you. Boundaries are usually not talked about, but they are clearly seen by others. By the way you dress and carry yourself, you can show others what your boundaries are. However, sometimes you will need to speak up. If someone acts like he doesn't understand or see your boundary lines, or if he says things like, "You turn me on when you smile," make sure you don't just pass it by. Say something like, "I don't appreciate that statement" or "That's not something you say to a friend." Use the opportunity to let others know where you stand. In most cases, though, you will show your boundary lines by the way you dress, speak to, respect, and honor others.

Don't be like those girls who go around the school and announce that they are virgins. Rather, live it out! Be a virgin physically, mentally, emotionally, and spiritually!

7. Find someone who can be your role model, mentor, and motivator.

Mentors are important in all of life. Look for an older woman in your church who can mentor you. She has to be someone who is spiritually and mentally mature and older than you. She needs to have a life that is praiseworthy before others and God. When you find a person who fits this description, go to her and tell her that you want her to mentor you in your Christian walk. Build a friendship with her first so that you can open up to her later at any time about any topic. And try to copy her lifestyle.

8. Stay away from places that can make you vulnerable to falling for the desires of your flesh.

Remember this: The number-one enemy of your soul is not the devil; rather, it is your flesh—the wrong desires and demands of your body. The Bible has one strategy for escaping destructive fleshly desires: "FLEE"!

Flee from sexual immorality. (1 Corinthians 6:18)

Flee the evil desires of youth and pursue righteousness, faith, love and peace, along with those who call on the Lord out of a pure heart. (2Timothy 2:22)

If your friends give you books to read or movies to watch that are not appropriate, say "No, thank you." Run away from those kinds of materials. Running away might mean never even opening that book, or staying away from the people who encourage you to follow their sinful lifestyles. If you find yourself in a situation where there's strong temptation to give in sexually, leave! Get out of that situation as fast as you can.

9. Watch what comes out of your mouth.

The Bible says this: "The mouth speaks out of that which fills the heart" (Matthew 12:34, NASB). Some people may say things like this: "I don't mean to curse or anything. It is just the word that is in my mouth." But your mouth is just an instrument of your heart and mind. Whatever is in your heart and mind comes out of your mouth. So always watch what you let your heart hold to or your mind meditate on.

Above all else, guard your heart, for everything you do flows from it. (Proverbs 4:23)

Life Principle:

"An idle mind is the devil's workshop." (English Proverb)
"Stand guard at the door of your mind every day." (Jim Rohn)

Guarding your mind is guarding your whole life, because every destructive habit and sinful lifestyle first gets conceived in the mind. As you pay close attention to what is going on in your mind, you won't be caught off guard by what your body chooses to do.

Assignment:

The assignments given in this book can be done individually or together with your CG-STAT group.

If a girl sleeps with a guy and ends up marrying the guy, is she still considered a sinner? Doesn't God want her to have fun? Discuss this with your group, or write the answer in a journal. Use some of the Scriptures in this chapter to support your answer.

✿

CHAPTER ELEVEN

Sexual Purity Versus Sexual Immorality

Ruth is a very active eighteen-year-old girl. She is one of the choir members in her church and one of the leaders in the youth ministry. When she came to me for counseling, the first thing she said was, "I'm eighteen and I'm a virgin," and she giggled.

Not knowing why she wanted to see me, I said, "Good for you for keeping yourself from sex before marriage."

She quickly said, "Sexual purity is a big part of my life, and I've decided to stay a virgin until I get married."

Again, I said, "Good for you!"

Looking nervous, she said, "Can I ask you a question, though?"

I said, "Absolutely!"

"As I told you, I'm a virgin. My boyfriend and I decided not to have sex before marriage. But whenever we see each other, we love touching each other's bodies—I mean, *that place* too. Is that a wrong or sinful thing to do?"

Some kind of fear and nervousness took over her pretty face as she asked that question.

"Ruth, what is sexual purity?"

"Being a virgin, isn't it?" She looked more nervous than before.

"Ruth," I called her name and paused so that she could pull herself together. "Ruth, you are nervous now because even if you are a virgin, something is telling you that what you and your boyfriend are doing with each other is not right, and you can't find peace and rest in your soul about it. Am I right in my assumption?"

She nodded.

"You came to me to hear what I have to say about it?"

She nodded again.

"Ruth, sexual purity is more than being a virgin—" And I told Ruth the things you are about to read. So read carefully.

Sexual purity can be defined as keeping one's mind, emotions, body, and spirit from any sexual thoughts, activities, or sexual gratification or satisfaction before marriage.

Sexual immorality is just the opposite: it's any sexual activity done outside of marriage, either before or after.

Remember, sex was created by God to be practiced between one man and one woman within a marriage. Sexual satisfaction is holy and pleasurable for spirit, soul, and body, but *only* when it occurs in marriage. Outside marriage, any form of sex brings pain, agony, guilt, despair, stress, and depression. It can bring disease and even death. Because of what it does to the people of God, sex outside marriage is hated by God. It hurts his children and the fellowship he so desires to have with them. Since it is sin (something that is against the Word and the will of God), sex outside of marriage hurts people emotionally, mentally, physically, and spiritually.

But actually having sex isn't the only way to be sexually impure. Watching movies or reading books with sexual scenes, having unrestrained sexual fantasies, or getting involved in physical touch beyond holding hands and simple hello and good-bye kisses or hugs can all rob you of your sexual purity by making you vulnerable to sexual temptations. They make it easier to fall into sin when temptation comes. They expose you to actual sexually-immoral lifestyles that are beyond fantasies and dreams.

> But among you there must not be even *a hint* of sexual immorality, or of any kind of impurity, or of greed, because these are improper for God's holy people. (Ephesians 5:3, emphasis added)

As I told you before, sin starts in the mind and ends in physical expression. That is why Jesus said this:

> But I tell you that anyone who looks at a woman lustfully has already committed adultery with her in his heart. (Matthew 5:28)

That means that one can be physically a virgin but mentally and emotionally promiscuous.

In the sight of God, being a sexually pure person means being emotionally, mentally, physically, and spiritually pure. That may or may not include physical virginity.

That means sexual purity is more a condition of a person's heart than the actual outward evidence. For example, if a virgin and devoted Christian girl gets raped by her uncle or neighbor, it doesn't mean that she becomes a sexually immoral person before God. She is not physically a virgin, but she is still sexually pure before God.

The standard of God's sexual purity may sound "unachievable," and it is indeed an unachievable standard for us *if we try to do it by ourselves*—but God's grace, which we receive through believing in Jesus Christ, is with us to help us live the kind of life God expects us to live. This grace gives us the potential to reach to God's standard of sexual purity, and it makes it ours through Christ Jesus:

> For the grace of God has appeared that offers salvation to all people. It teaches us to say "No" to ungodliness and worldly passions, and to live self-controlled, upright and godly lives in this present age, while we wait for the blessed hope—the appearing of the glory of our great God and Savior, Jesus Christ, who gave himself for us to redeem us from all wickedness and to purify for himself a people that are his very own, eager to do what is good. (Titus 2: 11–14)

Not only do we have God's grace, but we also have his mercy and spirit through his Son, Jesus Christ:

> My dear children, I write this to you so that you will not sin. But if anybody does sin, we have an advocate with the Father—Jesus Christ, the Righteous One. (1 John 2:1)

> If you love me, keep my commands. And I will ask the Father, and he will give you another advocate to help you and be with you forever— the Spirit of truth. The world cannot accept him, because it neither sees him nor knows him. But you know him, for he lives with you and will be in you. (John 14:15-17)

> If you stumble and fall, God's mercy is always there to clean you up from all your sins. He will make you brand-new, a virgin in his sight. He restores you and your life.

If we confess our sins, he is faithful and just and will forgive us our sins and purify us from all unrighteousness. (1 John 1:9)

Yes, once you lose your virginity physically, you can't be a virgin again. But in the sight of God, once you confess your sin, forsake your sinful ways, and turn to God, you are seen by him as a completely clean, pure, and virgin girl all over again. P. B. Wilson calls this "secondary virginity" in her book, *Your Knight in Shining Armor.*

Remember one last, important point: It is not virginity that entitles you to be called a child of God, but being found in his Son, Jesus Christ. Yes, being a virgin while seeking the will of God is like winning the "double jeopardy" points in the game of life. Being a virgin won't add anything to God, but it will add something to you! By being a virgin for all of your single years, all the joy and mental, spiritual, and physical protection belongs to you. That is why God instructs us to walk in his ways so that it will be well with us.

Obey me, and I will be your God and you will be my people. Walk in obedience to all I command you, that it may go well with you. (Jeremiah 7:23)

If you keep my commands, you will remain in my love, just as I have kept my Father's commands and remain in his love. I have told you this so that my joy may be in you and that your joy may be complete. (John 15:10-11)

It is the will and desire of God for us to enjoy life to the fullest, but apart from him and apart from his Word, we are like untrained passengers trying to fly an airplane without a trained pilot on board. That will end in disaster!

It is critical for you to have a personal relationship with Christ Jesus, who is "the trained pilot" on board your airplane. He is the only one who led a perfect life, and he is the only one who can enable you to live a life that honors God, yourself, and others. He is also the only one who can restore your life when you mess it up.

You Are the Temple of God

Anything that is short of sexual purity is sexual immorality. Sexual immorality is sin before God. If you find yourself in anything that is not honorable to God and that doesn't equate to sexual purity, confess it quickly to God and do everything you can to stay away from it.

Sexual sin, according to the Bible, is seen by God differently than other sins. Why?

Look at these Bible verses:

> *Do you not know that your bodies are members of Christ himself? Shall I then take the members of Christ and unite them with a prostitute? Never!* Do you not know that he who unites himself with a prostitute is one with her in body? For it is said, "The two will become one flesh." But whoever is united with the Lord is one with him in spirit. *Flee from sexual immorality. All other sins a person commits are outside the body, but whoever sins sexually, sins against their own body.* Do you not know that your bodies are temples of the Holy Spirit, who is in you, whom you have received from God? You are not your own; you were bought at a price. Therefore honor God with your bodies. (1 Corinthians 6:15–18, emphasis added)

Jesus died for you so that you would be saved from hell—eternal separation from God. God sent his Son as a ransom for you so that you can come to him. Once you are his, your body is his. He will use all the "members" of your body—that means your body parts, like arms, legs, tongue, ears, and eyes—to reach this dark world. Your body is an instrument of righteousness.

As the above Bible passage says, sexual sin is done against our own bodies. All other sins are done outside of our bodies.

Let me give you one example: If John killed Raymond, who sinned against who? John killed Raymond. Sin has been committed, and that sin is murder. John did that sin against Raymond. John didn't die; only Raymond did.

But when we sin sexually, it is completely different. Let's say John slept with a girl he isn't married to. Sin has been committed; the sin of sexual immorality. But John committed the sin against his own body. The girl also sinned against her body.

If these people are born-again Christians, their bodies, as the Bible says, are the temple of God—God purchased their bodies by the blood of Jesus to make them his temple, his house. Sexual sin is an attack against the temple of the Lord!

> Do not offer the parts of your body to sin, as instruments of wickedness, but rather offer yourselves to God, as those who have been brought from death to life; and offer the parts of your body to him as instruments of righteousness. (Romans 6:13)

Furthermore, since your body is God's temple, God will fight against you when you agree with the desire of your flesh to sin against your body and destroy his temple. Yes, sexual sin is a personal issue to God! Look at the following Bible verses:

Don't you know that you yourselves are God's temple and that God's Spirit dwells in your midst? *If anyone destroys God's temple, God will destroy that person; for God's temple is sacred, and you together are that temple.* (1 Corinthians 3:16–17, emphasis added)

Who can fight and win against God? No one! So choose to stay away from sexual immorality. As the Bible says, always choose to flee away, even from the temptation.

And always remember this: God is always on your side. He fights for you so that you will have abundant life. He fights against anything and anybody that comes to destroy his daughter—you!

God has so many purposes for sex and marriage! They reflect the perfect union of Jesus and the church. They point to the coming of Jesus to be married to his Bride. A man and a woman, joined in marriage according to the Word of God, are one in serving God. They seek his will together and strive to know him more and raise their children for him. God uses that union to raise a generation that will worship him in Spirit and in truth and to reach out and save the lost. When married couples have sex, they are accomplishing God's purpose—they are actually doing his work.

Can you imagine the consequences of destroying all these plans and purposes of God? It is huge!

Sexual immorality can even lead to death. Read 2 Samuel 11 and 12, about the story of King David's adultery and the deaths that resulted from it. Read Judges 16 to see what led to the death of a strong and anointed warrior, Samson.

Life Principle:

Sin is never barren! All fully-grown sin gives birth to death!

Sin gives birth to death. That death may come in different forms and shapes. One who is sexually impure may lose her marriage, another may lose her opportunity to meet a man who could be her husband; others may become diseased or die.

> When tempted, no one should say, "God is tempting me."
> For God cannot be tempted by evil, nor does he tempt any-
> one; but each person is tempted when they are dragged away
> by their own evil desire and enticed. Then, after desire has
> conceived, it gives birth to sin; and sin, when it is full-grown,
> gives birth to death. (James 1:13–15)

Notice something here: Confessing your sin will free you from the guilt and penalty of your sin (eternal death), but it may not free you from all the consequences of your sin.

We will meet Samson and King David in heaven, but both of them suffered because of the consequences of their sexual sin.

In this day and age, sexually transmitted diseases are more than we can count on our fingers. Some of them, such as AIDS, cause death; some of them, such as herpes, do not have a cure.

One cannot pick and choose which consequence of sin to have. One dies from a sexually immoral lifestyle, others live with a disease that doesn't have a cure, and still others live with mental and emotional disturbances that resulted from sexual immorality.

> Marriage *is to be held* in honor among all, and the *marriage*
> bed *is to be* undefiled; for fornicators and adulterers God will
> judge. (Hebrew 13:4, NASB)

I once heard some young people say this: "I've already committed too much sin for me to stop the consequences. So I might as well continue to live in it. It won't get any worse than it already is."

Actually, it will get worse if you continue sinning.

If you are exposed to fire and manage to get out with only first degree-burns, would you go back into the fire thinking that since the fire already got you the first time, now you're safe? I bet you wouldn't, unless you are mentally ill.

The Bible actually equates sleeping around to walking on hot coals or scooping fire into your lap. Do you think you can come out of that without getting burned? No way!

Can a man scoop fire into his lap
  without his clothes being burned?
Can a man walk on hot coals
  without his feet being scorched?
So is he who sleeps with another man's wife;
  no one who touches her will go unpunished.
(Proverbs 6:27–29)

The best strategy to keep from getting burned by fire is to stay away from it. It is the same with sexual sin. FLEE! Flee from it today, now, not tomorrow, not later, but now!

Life Principle:

No action without a reaction; no sin without a consequence.
"A *journey* of a *thousand miles* begins with a single step."
(Lao-tzu)

Do not be deceived, God is not mocked; for whatever a man sows, this he will also reap. (Galatians 6:7)

There is one other important truth I don't want you to miss here. People don't get themselves into a lifestyle that will destroy their lives in one day. Rather, a little compromise here and a little compromise there will eventually get them there. Usually they'll reach that point before they know it.

I remember a beautiful song I heard a few years back. The song is called "Slow Fade" by Casting Crowns. It goes like this:

It's a slow fade when you give yourself away
It's a slow fade when black and white have turned to gray
Thoughts invade, choices are made, a price will be paid
When you give yourself away
People never crumble in a day
It's a slow fade, it's a slow fade

"People never crumble in a day." This is so true. Nobody gets up one morning and decides to lead a sexually promiscuous lifestyle or to become a drug addict. Rather, one seemingly small wrong choice leads to another until a life has been ruined.

If your spirit is telling you that it's wrong music you're listening to, or a wrong crowd you're hanging out with, or a wrong intimate phone conversation you're having with a guy, or a wrong chat you're exchanging over the Internet, stop it immediately. Don't say, "I'll stop it tomorrow." Don't trust yourself for tomorrow. If you can't do it today, what makes you think you can do it tomorrow?

If your Christian friends warn you of the wrong steps you're taking, or your parents, siblings, or people who care about you say something like, "I don't think I like your friendship with so-and-so. She is a bad influence," listen to them and take action immediately.

No, you won't crumble in a day. But wrong choices will lead to crumbling eventually.

Assignment:

The assignments given in this book can be done individually or together with your CG-STAT group.

1. If you sin against God in any way, what do you need to do to receive the forgiveness of God in your life? Refer to the following Bible verses to answer the question. Write down your answers on a paper and read it to yourself and see if it makes sense in light of these Bible verses. If you are in the CG-STAT program, make sure you share your answer with the group and hear how others answered the question differently or similar to yours and learn from each other.

If we confess our sins, He is faithful and righteous to forgive us our sins and to cleanse us from all unrighteousness. (1 John 1:9, NASB)

Whoever conceals their sins does not prosper, but the one who confesses and renounces them finds mercy. (Proverbs 28:13)

2. What were the consequences of David's sin?

Read 2 Samuel 11 and 12 and write your answer in a journal. If you are in CG-STAT program, make sure you compare your answers with others to see if you miss anything.

※

CHAPTER TWELVE

The Power of Modesty

Hanna is a straight-A student with a natural gift for memorizing anything. She was one of the two students from her high school who were elected to take part in the National Vocabulary Championship. When I met Hanna, she was in a group Bible study I was invited to speak to on the life of Esther (the story you find in the book of Esther, in the Bible). At the end of our discussion, while I was gathering my stuff to leave, she stayed with me, helping me pack my things.

I said, "I heard that you are a straight-A student and have an excellent memory. Good for you!"

Without any exaggeration or excitement, she said, "Thank you."

"I'm sure you know the whole Bible by heart now, don't you?"

Smiling, she said, "I memorized quite a few verses, but not the whole Bible."

"So how is that helping you so far in your life?" I asked.

She paused to think about it. "You know what? It is helping me a lot, but these days I am getting a little confused about something."

"About what?" I asked.

She replied, "I'm sixteen, and I don't have a plan to date until I turn seventeen or eighteen. But these days, most guys in my school are asking me for a date now. And the funny thing is, these guys are not Christians. I'm not sure why they are interested in me instead of my friends."

I quickly said, "Well, it is obvious that you are cuter and smarter than your friends."

"Well," she said, smiling, "one of my friends said I'm attracting all these guys with my miniskirt, but I totally disagree with her."

Aha! That brought some new understanding to the conversation. "Hanna, I'm not sure how short your miniskirts are, but I know this much. Wearing a miniskirt may make you feel free and beautiful, but your exposed thighs may attract the guys to you more than you may want to. When you expose yourself that much, you may attract a guy who is more interested in touching your thigh than knowing you as a person."

"Ew!" she said.

Smiling, I nodded with agreement as if to say, "You bet it's ew!"

The way you dress matters. Dressing modestly can help you to live a life of sexual purity, and it will help the guys around you keep their own thoughts pure. It can also open the door for you to speak to others about God. By the way you dress, people may dare to assume things about you and your moral values that do not really represent you.

You may say "Who cares?", but if you are a child of God, you should care about how other people see you, because you are God's ambassador.

We are therefore Christ's ambassadors. (2 Corinthians 5:20)

As a rule of thumb, ask yourself this question before you decide to put clothes on: *Is this the way I want to represent my God to the watching world?* The Bible says that we who believe in Jesus are his ambassadors. We represent him in all areas of our lives, including the way we dress.

By the way you dress, you can communicate with others, without making any statement, about your moral values and boundaries. You represent who you are to others (at least as a first impression) by the way you dress and style yourself.

> I also want the women to dress modestly, with decency and propriety, adorning themselves, not with elaborate hair-styles or gold or pearls or expensive clothes, but with good deeds, appropriate for women who profess to worship God. (1Timothy 2:9–10)

There is a saying that goes like this: "Don't judge a book by its cover." It's a good saying, and true— as long as we use it for books! On the other hand, what you use to cover your body may speak volumes about you. In some cases, it may say something different from who you really are on the inside. The way you dress communicates to others whether you want to be respected or not.

A girl who wears clothes appropriately sends a message like this: "I respect you, and I need you to respect me."

The way you adorn yourself sends a message to guys who are looking at you. It may send a message like, "This is my body. If you want to play with it, you can." Or it may send the opposite message such as, "I am beautiful, but I am not cheap."

Remember, you may send a message you don't intend to. It's important to know what messages certain kinds of clothing send!

The choice is yours whether to invite a guy to sin or to call him to purity.

You may say, "But I like to express myself with very tight clothes and very short skirts, and it is not my intention to send any signal to anybody. I just like this style, and I think it looks cute on me."

But remember this: you are called to walk in love, and if you walk in a way that causes your brother to stumble, you are not walking in love. If a boy sins in his mind by lusting after your body that is exposed for everyone to see, he will be guilty of sinning against God.

> Anyone who looks at a woman lustfully has already committed adultery with her in his heart. (Matthew 5:28)

I know, you are not called to sanctify and purify anybody. Ultimately, it's up to guys what they do with their eyes and their minds. But at the same time, you're called not to be a reason for anyone to stumble in sin. It's your job to love the guys in your life by presenting yourself in a way that calls for respect, not lust.

> If anyone causes one of these little ones—those who believe in me—to stumble, it would be better for them if a large millstone were hung around their neck and they were thrown into the sea. (Mark 9:42)

Life Principle
"Modesty is not only an ornament, but also a guard to virtue." (Joseph Addison)

The best way to show the watching world that you respect and honor yourself and others is by wearing appropriate and modest clothing. By not wearing modest clothes, you show those around you that you don't honor or respect yourself, God, or others.

It is very hard for a boy to keep himself from staring and flirting with a girl who doesn't guard herself by dressing modestly, especially for a boy who is not spiritually mature enough to bounce his eyes away from a girl's body.

Some boys may do or say anything to get what they want from a girl. They are not mentally-dead creatures, but their sexual desire can take over above and beyond any reasoning or logical thinking they may have.

A boy who is not restrained by the Holy Spirit may treat you like a princess until he gets what he wants. After that, you are just another girl. That is why they say, "Men give love to get sex, and girls give sex to get love."

Wearing clothes that appropriately cover your body will not make you popular with everyone—definitely not!—but at the same time, you will send a signal that you are not a sex toy for any guy to play with. Boys exist who are living holy lives and who want a healthy, God-honoring relationship with a girl. You just have to pray that God will let one of these guys' path cross yours. And know this: Most of the time, men get attracted to a girl of their own type!

Personal physical boundaries can get blurry because of immodesty. You don't have to go around your school and say to the boys "You can't hug me this way" or "You can't come closer to me than this" to let them know that you're pursuing a sexually pure life. By the way you dress and act around boys, you communicate to them what you're after and how you want to be treated.

Don't forget this: Before people hear what you have to say or what you stand for, they will see what you look like—how you are dressed and how you present yourself.

You may feel like dressing up like in ways that feel good to you. But not everything that feels good is right. Don't let your feelings lead your life. Instead, let the Word of God and the Spirit of God lead your life. Remember that you are the Lord's temple, and his Spirit will lead you even in details such as what to wear and what not to wear.

> For those who are led by the Spirit of God are the children of God. (Romans 8:14)

To be "led by the Holy Spirit" means to lead your life according to the Word of God. Hide the Word of God in your heart, and you will find him leading your way.

> Your word is a lamp for my feet, a light on my path.
> (Psalm 119:105)

You may hear girls say things like this: "Then, *suddenly*, he started kissing me." There is no "suddenly" in most life occurrences, except for real accidents, or in cases of abuse. As long as you dress in a way to reveal your body inappropriately, you allow yourself to be seen as an "easy target" or as a "sex object" for some boys. You are not responsible for what others choose to do, but you *are* responsible for the way you dress yourself and the signals you send.

Dressing modestly is a guard to virtue because it sends a signal that you are not to be treated disrespectfully.

Life Principle
Not everything that feels good is necessarily good.

> "I have the right to do anything," you say—but *not everything is beneficial.* "I have the right to do anything"—but I will not be mastered by anything." (1 Corinthians 6:12, emphasis added)

"I have the right to do anything," you say—but not everything is beneficial. "I have the right to do anything"—but *not everything is constructive.*" (1 Corinthians 10:23, emphasis added)

Life Principle:

Your body is the temple of the Holy Spirit.

Do you not know that *your bodies are temples of the Holy Spirit,* who is in you, whom you have received from God? You are not your own; you were bought at a price. Therefore honor God with your bodies. (1 Corinthians 6:19–20, emphasis added)

Assignment:

The assignments given in this book can be done individually or together with your CG-STAT group.

For the next class, read the Book of Esther and answer the following questions:

1. Who was Esther's parent or guardian in the story, and what was his number-one style of parenting Esther?
2. Other than being strikingly beautiful, what were Esther's good qualities of manner, behavior, and attitude? What was Esther's source of strength? Write your answer in your journal and read the Book of Esther again to see if you are missing anything. If you are part of the CG-STAT group, discuss your answer in the next class.

CHAPTER THIRTEEN

Having a Boyfriend

Abigail is a sixth grader. She sits in her class just next to the outside window where she has a good view of the school sports field and the forest just next to it.

This class has been a different class for Abigail even though she still has almost all of her fifth-grade classmates. It's different for one major reason. She has a crush on one of her classmates, Mike, who sits two rows in front of her. She speaks with him during recess or in class when she gets a chance, but most of the time she looks through the classroom window and enjoys daydreaming about Mike and her being singers, in a concert hall, singing a romantic song while everybody is cheering and dancing to the music.

Dreaming of having a boyfriend is a common dream for girls this age. It's normal and natural! As the Bible teaches, there is a time for everything.

There is a time for everything, and a season for every activity under the heavens. (Ecclesiastes 3:1)

Just as there is a right time to eat and a right time to go to sleep and a right time to go to school and a right time to stay home, there is also a right time to have a boyfriend.

If there is a right time for these things, there is also a wrong time for them!

If you see someone sleeping at 11 a.m., you will probably think that they are sick. If they are adults, you think that they worked the night shift and are catching up on their sleep. Eleven a.m. is not the right time to sleep.

Once you have entered puberty, thinking of having a boyfriend is part of a normal developmental process. However, if you are still in middle school, junior high, or your early high school years, this is not the time for a boyfriend, nor is it the right time for you to dwell on the thought of having a boyfriend or getting a date. Remember what I said earlier: If you're given to a thought and dwell on it (whether the thought is right or wrong), it is only a matter of time before you act on it. On the other side, what the mind agrees on, the body can't oppose!

The Bible says this:

> But each person is tempted when they are dragged away by their own evil desire and enticed. Then, after desire has conceived, it gives birth to sin; and sin, when it is full-grown, gives birth to death. (James 1:14–15)

The number-one thing you need to watch out for is what you let your mind meditate on.

You may find yourself interested in reading love stories or watching romantic movies. It's okay to read and watch those stories as long as they are "clean," without sexual scenes or references.

However, just because you think about romance or you become interested in reading and watching love stories doesn't mean that you're mentally, physically, and emotionally ready to be in a relationship with a boy.

Before you get involved in a relationship, it is good to know guys as friends. The way you act around your friends who are boys should be different than the way you act around your friends who are girls. Why? Because, remember, guys are sexually wired differently than girls. You want to treat them with real love and respect by observing boundaries, dressing modestly, and keeping some emotional distance.

When You're Ready to Date . . .

When you get to the age of dating, around seventeen or eighteen, it is very important to let your Christian moral values be obvious to the guy who wants to date you. How? First, of course, by the way you dress and behave.

And then, before you go on a date, invite him to meet your parents.

Do you know why? A guy who is looking for someone to take advantage of probably won't accept your invitation to come over to your parents' house to meet them. He may respond to your request like this: "Are you from the sixteenth century? You don't need your parents' approval to go on a date! Am I your very first date and you're scared? Come on, now. Grow up!"

Taking this step actually shows that you're a grown girl who is wise and mature enough to take the narrow road to protect herself from common traps many have fallen into. It shows that you respect yourself and your parents and that you are loved and protected by them.

When your parents meet a guy, they can judge from his approach and attitude whether he is worthy to go out with their daughter or not. Remember, your parents love you and care for you. Listening to them can save you from lots of heartaches and hurts down the road!

One piece of wrong thinking many girls face is this: "I am not worthy of having this guy as a date. Who am I to ask him to meet my parents? I am lucky that he asked me, and I won't demand anything from him except being his date."

My dear, if this kind of thinking ever comes to you, please remember this: You are precious daughter of God! God is the King of Kings. If he is your Father, what does that make you? A princess! That is how God and all the hosts of heavenly angels see you. Please know who you are in Christ!

Let's say the cutest guy at school asks you out. Don't ever think that you are lucky to be asked by him! Having the right identity in Christ Jesus will make you strong enough not to be seriously attracted to a guy who has good physical features but lacks all the character and traits you're looking for. You see, if you know your identity, you will pay more attention to his character and faith in Christ than to his physical features. It is nice to be the girlfriend of the cutest guy in the school, but it's worth nothing if he doesn't value you as a person and respect your stand in life.

Remember, you are a princess, a child of God—a God who is King of kings and Lord of lords! A princess should marry a prince. Don't settle for anything less!

If you are seventeen or eighteen, I highly advise you to read books on Christian dating written by Christian authors, books such as *The Ten Commandments of Dating* by Ben Young and Dr. Samuel Adams and *Boy Meets Girl: Say Hello to Courtship* by Joshua Harris.

Remember, a joyful life won't just come from heaven. It requires careful and thorough planning, strategy, wise counseling, reading, preparation, and wise choices.

When it comes time for you to start dating, ask advice from the people you respect, mentally and spiritually.

> For lack of guidance a nation falls, but victory is won
> through many advisers. (Proverbs 11:14)

Remember this: Life is full of choices and decisions. Your present choices and decisions determine the next chapter of your life. So make sure you take it seriously.

There is a right way and a wrong way of dating; there is a right way of choosing a life partner and a wrong way of doing it.

Earlier I said that you didn't pick your parents and they didn't pick you. It is God who authors the child/parent relationship. However, in the case of marriage (which is your ultimate reason for dating), you have a choice. That is why the Bible says this:

> He who finds a wife finds what is good and receives favor
> from the LORD. (Proverbs 18:22)

That means dating (or courting) is a process of finding Mr. Right.

At your age, it is easy to think that the first guy you like is the one you're ultimately going to marry. Rest assured of this: That may happen one time in thousands. Chances are you will meet and like a number of guys before you meet the one you decide to marry.

Therefore, keep in mind: When you are ready for dating, the first guy you date will probably not be your husband. Keep that in mind, and make decisions that are wise. No matter what, though, it won't hurt if you first invite him home to meet your parents!

The Ultimate Goal

For a Christian, dating has one ultimate goal, and that goal is to find a life partner, a person you will eventually marry and live the rest of your life with.

You see, dating just for the sake of dating or because others are doing it is completely wrong for you. It will lead you to a path of destruction.

Knowing that dating has an ultimate goal will make you careful as to who you go out with. You won't waste your time with a person you have no intention of pursuing a lifelong relationship with. It is good to give a guy a chance to prove himself to you, to show that he is worthy of having you as a date and eventually making you his wife, but if you already know that he doesn't have the major qualifications you're looking in a man—for example, if you know for sure that he is not a believer in Christ Jesus—then it is not good for you to spend time with him. Otherwise, little by little, he can lead you to join him.

Do not be misled: "Bad company corrupts good character." (1 Corinthians 15:33)

Do not be yoked together with unbelievers. For what do righteousness and wickedness have in common? Or what fellowship can light have with darkness? (2 Corinthians 6:14)

The take-home message here is this: When you get to the right age, date to look for Prince Charming, your future husband, and *not* because everybody else is doing it!

Life Principle
There is a right time for everything!

There is a time for everything, and a season for every activity under the heavens . . . He has made everything beautiful in its time." (Ecclesiastes 3:1, 11)

Life Principle:

Be cautious of the easy and quick thing!

The Bible identifies two opposite ways:

Enter through the narrow gate. For wide is the gate and
broad is the road that leads to destruction, and many enter
through it. But small is the gate and narrow the road that
leads to life, and only a few find it. (Matthew 7:13–14)

Your choice can lead you to life or death, so choose wisely!

This day I call the heavens and the earth as witnesses against
you that I have set before you life and death, blessings and
curses. Now choose life, so that you and your children may
live." Deuteronomy 30:19

Choose life, especially when it comes to relationships. With
prayer, counseling, mentoring, and reading, you can always find
yourself choosing life over death.

Be open to receive advice from family members, church ministers, and authors of books about this topic. Surrounding yourself with wise counsel is always a smart move.

Listen to advice and accept discipline,
  and at the end you will be counted among the wise.
(Proverbs 19:20)

Assignment:

The assignments given in this book can be done individually or together with your CG-STAT group.

What do you think of the advice I give about dating? Write three or four benefits from doing dating right. If you are in a group, share your thoughts with each other.

༜

CHAPTER FOURTEEN

Frequently Asked Questions About Sex

In this chapter, you will find brief answers to some of the frequently asked questions in the area of sexuality. It is designed to give you a quick and brief reference to topics you may come across. I advise you to do further readings to get depth of knowledge on topics where you have more questions and interests.

What is orgasm?

Orgasm is the highest or most intense sexual excitement experience of sex. It is the peak of sexual excitation resulting from stimulation of private parts. This excitation point lasts an average of fifteen to thirty seconds.

Most young people are told that sex is all about achieving orgasm. However, this is false. Orgasm is just one part of sexual pleasure. The sexual pleasure God created for us gives pleasure, joy, and satiety before, during, and after orgasm or having sexual intercourse. This kind of sexual pleasure can only be achieved and experienced in the presence of God, and as you already know, God can't bless or participate in anything that doesn't uphold his standards of holiness.

Any sexual act that is not according to the plan and purpose of God leaves the user with more hunger and thirst for sexual fulfillment, which can't be quenched by anything or anyone. You see, when sex is practiced outside marriage, outside the will of God, it gives pleasure only to our flesh, leaving our spirit and soul hanging. Sex can only be truly pleasurable to our body, soul, and spirit when we have it in the boundary of God's will and purpose.

What is masturbation?

Masturbation is stimulating your sexual organ with a hand or devices called vibrators in order to achieve orgasm.

The Bible is silent regarding masturbation. However, that doesn't mean it is okay to do. As we have seen throughout this book, God is the creator of sex, sexual desire, and sexual pleasure. He gave us a "user's manual" that tells us what sex is for, when to do it, and with whom to do it.

Because we understand the purposes of sex as designed by God, we can see that masturbation is not a right or good activity. You see, masturbation is a technique to get sexual gratification outside the actual sexual act in a marriage between one man and one woman.

One thing to remember here is this: Masturbation is not sex! It is a technique or a method to get physical relief from sexual desire. The irony is that masturbation comes with emotional, mental, and spiritual bondage. Why? Because "masturbation does not satisfy sexual desires; it intensifies them" (*Every Young Woman's Battle* by Shannon Ethridge and Stephen Arterburn, p. 45.)

One may achieve orgasm through masturbation, but that only gives physical relief. Our spirit and soul also demand pleasure, but they can't find it. That is why we don't hear anyone who is a born-again, committed follower of Jesus Christ saying that they feel good about themselves after they masturbate. No, they feel dirty, empty, and usually guilty. Why? It is because masturbation leaves the soul and spirit hanging, hungry for pleasure.

Sex is not just about physical relief. It is also about sexual joy and the pleasure of our soul, body, and spirit, which only happens when sex occurs as God planned it in his presence. People who masturbate may be misled by the idea that they will be able to quench their sexual desires in this way. That being the main goal, most of them quickly move to using pornographic websites, movies, magazines, toys, and other similar materials to get what they are aiming for. They may increase the number of times they masturbate in a day. But regardless of their efforts, sexual pleasure and joy will remain a fantasy for them.

One more thing: Sex, as God created it, is something spouse gives to spouse. It is not something to be taken, but given. Masturbation works on the principle of selfishness. People masturbate to get pleasure, to themselves, by themselves. Sex, according to God, is something one gives and in return receives from a spouse.

> The wife does not have authority over her own body but
> yields it to her husband. In the same way, the husband does
> not have authority over his own body but yields it to his wife.
> (1 Corinthians 7:4)

Therefore as a child of God, masturbation is something you need to stay away from. If you are already in it, seek help to be free from it.

Is masturbation a sin?

Sin starts in the mind. Ask yourself this question before you say whether masturbation is a sin or not: "Why do I need to masturbate?"

As a single person, your sexual desire is there for a purpose. God doesn't create a desire not to meet it. Your sexual desire, as a single person, is a reminder that you need to prepare yourself for your future husband. Singlehood is a reminder that it is not good to be alone. It teaches you how to trust and depend on God to meet all your needs and desires at the appropriate time, a time God himself sets for you, a time perfect for your body, soul, and spirit.

With that in mind, you be the judge: Do you think giving yourself to the desire of your flesh for sexual satisfaction right now is a right thing for a child of God?

The initial interest of finding pleasurable feeling by touching private parts is innocent, but becoming engaged in finding sexual pleasure through masturbation will eventually pave the way into a disobedient and sinful lifestyle. Please stay away from it.

How far is too far? How far does a Christian couple have to stay away from physical touch?

"How far can I go with my boyfriend without disobeying God?" is a very common question.

Anything that interferes with what you know about the truth of God, and anything that interferes with the peace of your conscience, should be kept away from.

Any form of physical touch to express love or to trigger a sexual response from the other person, even if those actions are not sinful by themselves, can lead you to a sinful act from which you as a single person need to stay away. Remember the rule of sexual temptation: FLEE.

Whenever you say no to any sinful act, you are honoring God in your life. When you honor God, God is always quick to honor you.

But now the LORD declares: "Far be it from me! Those who honor me I will honor, but those who despise me will be disdained." (1 Samuel 2:30)

You see, whenever you obey God and stay away from the things that can hurt you and your fellowship with him, you are saying to God: "Lord, you know what is best for me. I don't know what is good for me. The only thing I know is this: whatever you said is good is good for me. Though I sometimes don't understand your ways, I choose to stick with them."

That is honoring God! You are saying, "God, you are God; and I am human." Humble yourself to the lordship of Jesus in your life, and he will honor you in due time.

Humble yourselves, therefore, under God's mighty hand, that he may lift you up in due time. (1 Peter 5:6)

If you do the opposite, you are saying to God: "I know what is best for me. Stay away from me because I don't like what you choose for me."

Is it okay to kiss my boyfriend?

One of the most common questions I've received so far from young girls (boys as well), after I taught about sexual purity, is this: Is it okay to kiss my boy/girlfriend?

This is my answer: If Jesus considers "looking at a girl lustfully" as adultery (Matthew 5:28), what makes you think that kissing, exchanging saliva, one of the fluids of the body to bring one man and one woman into oneness in marriage, will be "an okay" thing to do? What do those two people (one man and one woman) who are kissing passionately think during or after kissing? How do their bodies react to that kissing?

Whenever I ask these questions, I always get a look that says, "Oh, I didn't connect those dots before."

Our body is created in a way to respond to sexual stimuli or triggers such as kissing. Kissing has a place and a role. It is one of the ways married couples express their love to each other, and it is one of the ways they invite each other into a sexual union. It is a wonderful gift a wife can give to her husband and the husband to his wife.

You know that we have nerves all over our bodies, in and outside. These nerves transport messages to the brain and back to the body parts where they are located. Nerves that are found immediately under our skin, for example, enable us to feel, understand, and know when we are touched, or when we get hurt. They let the brain know of the fact so fast that when we cut our finger, for example, we immediately feel the pain.

Well, did you know that we also have nerves on our lips? These nerves are similar to the nerves found on our sexual organs. When they are touched in the heat of attraction, they send a message to the brain to send out sexual hormones to prepare the body for the anticipated sex to follow.

I know, not everyone has sex right after they kiss—but everyone will find themselves fighting the urge to have sex. That urge is created by the powerful sexual hormones that are secreted in the body after kissing. Eventually these hormones win!

The lips are not the only thing to get involved in a kiss. Heartbeat, blood pressure, and minds are involved in the process. Heart rate and blood pressure increase as the brain orders the body to be ready for sex as it secretes sex hormones. Sexual organs are also involved and change in size as they prepare themselves for anticipated sex.

Do you see how passionate kissing leads a person into sin?

So whenever young people ask me if kissing is a sin or not, my simple answer is always: Keep your first kiss for the night of your wedding!

Who can I let touch my body? Is it okay to be free with my cousins who are boys?

You should not let anyone touch you in ways that make you feel uncomfortable. Don't let anyone brush up against your body, grab you, or pat you in ways that make you feel violated.

Nobody has a right to touch your body inappropriately. Your doctor can touch your body, at the permission of you and your parents, for the purpose of a physical checkup or treatment. If you feel like someone is touching you inappropriately, make sure you speak first to your parents or pastor. Do not keep secret about this. If at any time you find yourself in a dangerous environment, for example, if you find yourself with a guy in a secluded area and you feel like you are trapped and feel fearful, do not even think for a second. Call the police.

Is it okay for me to date an unbeliever since I may decide not to marry him?

This is a very important question many teens and young people in their twenties are asking. The Bible is clear in this regard:

Do not be yoked together with unbelievers. For what do righteousness and wickedness have in common? Or what fellowship can light have with darkness? What harmony is there between Christ and Belial? Or what does a believer have in common with an unbeliever? (2 Corinthians 6:14–15)

When you are old and mature enough to date (your parents should advise you about this, and give you permission to start dating when they think you are ready), the first important thing for you, daughter of God, to know is this: Dating has a goal. That goal is to find Mr. Right, the man with whom you will lead your life until death do you part. So you shouldn't date *anybody* just for the sake of dating.

When I ask how their relationship with their boyfriend is going, some girls respond like this: "He is not a believer. I'm just having fun. It is not serious."

It is not wise for you to date an unbeliever assuming that it won't become a serious relationship! Actually, this kind of relationship has a tendency to become a serious one—serious enough to lead you to a life of disobedience against God, your parents, and your own faith and conviction. So it is always wise to stay away from dating an unbeliever, or even a person who professes to be a believer but doesn't have a Christ-like lifestyle.

After all, before you even entertain the idea of going out for a cup of coffee with a guy, your first requirement should be that he is a sincere and genuine believer in Christ Jesus. If he doesn't meet your first requirement, why do you entertain the rest of his qualities and spend time with him? There's no point!

Some girls say, "But he doesn't smoke; he doesn't drink alcohol or anything. He doesn't believe in sex before marriage or sleeping around."

Remember this: It doesn't matter what he believes or doesn't believe, or what kind of quality characteristics he may exhibit, if he doesn't believe in Christ, or live a Christ-like life, you have no business with him.

Compromising on your first criterion is like compromising in the foundation of a million-dollar house. It may be worth a million dollars, but if its foundation is not firm and secure enough for it to stand for many years, you shouldn't invest in it. It is just a matter of time before that mansion crumbles. Just like that, eventually you will find out that you and your unbelieving boyfriend can't go together any longer. Your relationship will eventually crumble—or else your relationship with God will.

So heed this advice in your heart: The Word of God is true all the time, through all generations and at all seasons! If it says "Do not be yoked with an unbeliever," then don't go on getting yoked with one. Flee!

Is oral sex sin?

Oral sex can be defined as touching each other's sexual organs with the mouth for the purpose of having orgasm. That means the male sex organ doesn't go into the girl's private part. Many teenage girls think that oral sex is okay since sexual organs are not involved in the act and they are able to keep their virginity.

But do you remember what we said earlier regarding any sexual activities before marriage? Yes, any activities that are sexual in nature are considered sexual immorality before marriage, and it is very important to flee from each and every one of these acts, including doing, watching, reading, or hearing sexually explicit materials.

Is it okay to have "hand work" without being involved in the actual sexual act?

"Hand work" can be defined as touching each other's sexual organs with a hand to bring each other to orgasm.

The answer I gave for the above question is applicable here as well.

The Bible says this: "But among you *there must not be even a hint of sexual immorality*, or of any kind of impurity, or of greed, because these are improper for God's holy people" (Ephesians 5:3, emphasis added).

Is it okay to date a man I met online?

The only evidence you have that a person you met online is who he says he is through his writings and pictures posted online. Anybody can write in ways that make them look and sound like a genuine Christian, and anyone can post the best picture ever. Tragically, girls have been sexually assaulted, abducted, and even killed, by young men or older men, who allured them by posting false pictures.

There is no reason to believe this kind of story can't happen to you. So it is a very wise idea to take extra precautions when it comes to online relationships.

In the chapter of this book called "Having a Boyfriend," you'll find a few principles you need to follow when you begin to date. One of these is to invite the young man you are planning to date home so he can meet your parents. This is one of the major filter techniques you need to implement in the process of dating to filter out the good guys from the bad ones.

The principle works for online relationships too. For your protection, make sure you get adults to meet him first. Use extra precaution if you meet someone online. Some girls prefer not to use online resources to find Prince Charming at all, and I can see why. The risk can be too high to gamble your life on.

If you have met someone online, and he wants to keep

something about himself a secret or tells you to keep it a secret, there is a good chance that he is hiding something from you that is very important for you to know.

Is it sin to have Facebook, Instagram, or similar social networking accounts?

Before answering this question, let's define sin. Sin is disobeying God's Word. It is anything that goes against the will of God.

There is nothing in the Bible that says networking sites are bad or sinful. In the same line of reasoning, however, there is no Bible quotation that says "Don't smoke cigarettes." Does that mean it's okay to smoke? The Bible does say that our body is the temple of the Lord and that we need to take care of it for the glory of God. Smoking cigarettes can cause lung cancer and other chronic pulmonary diseases which may disable a person for life or shorten the smoker's life altogether. By keeping our body healthy, we obey and worship God.

Having Facebook or other social networking accounts is not sin, but there are other questions you may need to answer before you decide whether to have an account or not (or whether to keep yours open!). As you read these questions, be honest with yourself!

How many hours do you spend on surfing on the Internet to keep your status update current and to keep yourself up-to-date about your contacts' updates and posts?

How much of your time is spent by being distracted as you receive texts or messages from your friends and contacts?

Is the time you spend on these social network sites worthwhile? It is helping you get where you want to be in life, spiritually, mentally, and economically?

When you compare the time you spend on the Internet with the time you spend before God, seeking his face, and reading and studying the Word of God, which one would you say is claiming you, your life, and your time the most?

I remember a familiar old Chinese saying that goes like this: "There is a good dog and a bad dog fighting within each of us. The one that is going to win is the one we feed the most."

It is best to know what you want to be in life and invest your time and energy accordingly.

Don't forget one more thing about these social networking sites: They can be addictive enough for you to stay away from anyone and everyone else, to the point of losing interest in doing anything other than being online surfing.

So be a judge of yourself as to how to balance social networking sites with your day-to-day, important life responsibilities and relationships. Just because everyone else has an account doesn't mean you need to have one. Just because everyone else has an account on every type of social media doesn't mean that you have to have all. Choose one or two social media, like Instagram, Twitter, or Facebook accounts where you can stay informed about the outside world, to keep in touch with your friends, and, of course, to have good networking skill with different people in the area of your interest.

If you have a tendency to be addicted to anything you land on, it is better to limit your engagement with social media and invest your time and energy on things that are worthy of it, such as your spiritual life and future career. If you decide to have one or two accounts, then have rules in place for yourself, such as these:

- My phone will be off after 6 p.m. so that I can spend time with my family, read the Bible, and pray without being distracted.
- I only surf online if I don't have anything to do.

- During school time, in class, and during study time, my phone is going to be off. If I need to use the Internet for school, I won't go to social networking sites.
- I don't need to respond to everyone's comment on my posts or comments.
- I don't need to update my status every day.
- Once or twice a day is enough times to check the sites.
- If I can't follow the rules I create for myself, I will delete my account and open one only when the time is right for me to have one.

You can add to this list, considering and asking yourself this important life issue: "Who do I want to be in life?" (Of course, the starting answer should be, "I want to be the person God created me to be, the person he wants me to be, the daughter of God, in speech, deeds, and thought life.")

Why is abortion a sin?

Abortion ends the life of a baby while he/she is in her mother's womb. Abortion is done by removing or forcing out the baby from the mother's womb by different techniques. If the pregnancy is early, abortion is done by giving the mother a drug that causes a miscarriage (medicine such as Plan B). If the pregnancy is in late term, abortion is done by burning the child alive with a saline solution, then by giving the mother a medicine to induce labor to deliver a burned and dead baby. The other technique is by reaching into the womb with surgical instrument and dismembering the child, and taking out the body parts of the baby one by one. At times, pieces of the baby's body might be left in the womb, which can cause a life threatening condition for the mother.

There is nothing good about abortion.

A woman may be forced or convinced to get an abortion for reasons such as being very young or not having the financial means to raise a child. Some women may decide to get an abortion because they think that if they get rid of the baby, they will live a carefree life. This is not true for most of the women who have an abortion. Guilt, shame, depression, despair, anxiety, fear, infertility, health problems, and long-term disability are just some of the consequences of abortion. Women must live with these, and they don't experience the carefree life they dreamt of having.

Abortion is wrong biblically because once a sperm fertilizes an egg, fertilization occurs within twenty-four hours of the union of sperm and egg, and the fertilized egg is a human being. God is making that amazing and precious baby in the womb from day one to nine months.

And killing that baby is wrong according to the Bible.

The word of the LORD came to me, saying,
"Before I formed you in the womb I knew you,
  before you were born I set you apart;
  I appointed you as a prophet to the nations."
                              (Jeremiah 1:4–5)

What will I do when God confronts me?
  What will I answer when called to account?
  Did not he who made me in the womb make them?
  Did not the same one form us both within our mothers?
                              (Job 31:14–15)

For you created my inmost being;
  you knit me together in my mother's womb.

I praise you because I am fearfully and wonderfully made;
   your works are wonderful,
   I know that full well. (Psalm 139:13–14)

In a partial-birth abortion, a baby who is in later stages of development is killed by sucking the baby's brain out while the baby is coming out of the mother's womb. There is yet another act of stopping the heart of a baby, which is known as born-alive abortion—killing babies who manage to survive abortion.

Remember this: As the mother of a baby, a woman shouldn't have a choice of letting the baby live or not. No one has that right. Rather, she has a choice to raise the baby herself or give the baby up for adoption. Always know this: If you or someone you know is facing a pregnancy crisis, you can find help from different Christian pregnancy centers that are established to help women and girls with unwanted pregnancy. You can find them in your state and even your city.

There is help out there. Millions and millions of people who can't have children because of health or barrenness are willing to take the baby. Here is one example of the websites to look for help: www.lifecall.org.

Two people may make a mistake and sleep together, but babies don't come by accident. Everyone is a creation of God, and God doesn't do anything by mistake or without purpose and plan.

Why is homosexuality a sin?

Although our society is very confused on this issue, if you understand God's purpose and plan for sex, it becomes very clear that homosexuality behavior does not fit that plan.

Nature itself tells us that two women or two men are not meant to be one in marital relationship. They cannot bring another human being to this world. Remember the 3 Ps of God's purpose for marriage? The first one is "propagate." According to the Bible, God created Adam and Eve and commanded them to multiply. There is no multiplication possible in a homosexual relationship.

Homosexuality is also mentioned in the Bible as one of the lifestyles of people who do not inherit the kingdom of God.

> Or do you not know that wrongdoers will not inherit the kingdom of God? Do not be deceived: Neither the sexually immoral nor idolaters nor adulterers nor men who have sex with men nor thieves nor the greedy nor drunkards nor slanderers nor swindlers will inherit the kingdom of God. *And that is what some of you were.* But you were washed, you were sanctified, you were justified in the name of the Lord Jesus Christ and by the Spirit of our God. (1 Corinthians 6:9–10, emphasis added)

That doesn't mean that a person who practices a homosexual lifestyle cannot come to the Lord. As you may notice from the above Bible verses, especially verse 11, some of the people who were born-again Christians in the Corinthian church were homosexuals.

A person who is already a born-again Christian may get tempted or fall into homosexuality; however, one can't be a born-again Christian and lead a homosexual lifestyle.

In the story of Sodom and Gomorrah in the book of Genesis chapter 19, you can read how God destroyed those cities mainly because of homosexual lifestyles. The truth of God stays the same throughout history. Nothing can change it!

If you or someone you know struggles with the sin of

homosexuality, seek help from your church ministers and other believers who may minister to others in this area.

What is a virgin?

The literal meaning of the word *virgin* is a person who has never had sexual intercourse. But the spiritual meaning of the word includes being a virgin mentally, spiritually, emotionally, and physically. One can get involved in oral sex and still remain physically a virgin, but in the eyes of God, that is not a complete picture of a virgin. On the other hand, one may get entangled in premarital sex and repent of their sin and become sexually pure. Those people will be seen by God just as if they were virgins.

Conclusion

My dear reader, thank you for reading through this book! As we conclude, let me ask you this question: Did you accept or agree with all the life standards in this book regarding how a Christian girl can please, honor, respect, and worship God in order to lead a life of true joy, pleasure, and happiness?

If you did, I encourage you to continue seeking the life that is pleasing to God by reading the Word of God, putting what you read and know in the Bible into practice, fellowshipping with other Christians, praying, and being involved in the ministry of the church.

If you are not sure about something you read here, I encourage you to read and study the Bible with other Bible-believing Christians and to read other books written by Christians about this topic.

If you did not have any teaching or counseling in this area before, and now you feel like you're too far gone to be saved by God, take heart. None of us can be too far away from the reach of the saving grace and power of Christ Jesus! This is true whether we are already Christians or whether we have not yet taken that step. The Bible says this:

> If we confess our sins, he is faithful and just and will forgive us our sins and purify us from all unrighteousness. (1 John 1:9)

My dear children, I write this to you so that you will not sin. But if anybody does sin, we have one who speaks to the Father in our defense—Jesus Christ, the Righteous One.

(1 John 2:1)

The devil is a liar. He lies and deceives to keep his victims away from the blessings of God. Once he gets them away, he keeps them there by accusing them of their sin, convincing them that there is no hope for them to go back where they used to be or to start afresh.

My dear, there is always hope for anyone who has breath in their lungs! If you are still breathing, you have hope in Christ to start again. He is a God of second chances.

Jesus Christ is your advocate, speaking to the Father on your behalf. Just come to him in prayer. If you are willing to pray with me, right now, let's do it. Here we go:

Dear Lord, I come to you today as I am, not able to change or do a thing in my life apart from your help and grace. I sinned against you by _____ (tell God what you did, naming your sins one by one). The Bible says that the blood of Jesus cleanses me from all my sins (1 John 1:7). Please cleanse me from all my sin and help me lead a life that is worthy of your calling. I want to obey you. Lord Jesus, you died for my sin, and now I want to live for you. Please help me. I pray this in the name of Jesus, amen.

This prayer is not a formula for a life that is pleasing to God, but it will help you begin the journey you are supposed to be on. You begin your journey by confessing your sins to God. That is the

first step! The second step is to turn your life 180 degrees and start
to go in the opposite direction, a direction for you to become the
person God wants you to be.

> He who conceals his sins does not prosper,
>> but whoever confesses and renounces them finds mercy.
>>> (Proverbs 28:13)

If you want to accept Jesus as your Savior for the first time, but
don't know how to do that, pray with me this prayer:

> Lord Jesus, I know I am a sinner, in need of a savior.
> I believe you died for me on the cross so that I might be
> saved. I ask you to forgive me of all my sins. I open my heart
> for you to come into my life, Lord Jesus.
> Right now I invite you to come to my heart as my Lord and
> Savior. Thank you, Father God, for forgiving me of all my
> sins and giving me eternal life
> I give my life to you. Help me to be the kind of person you
> want me to be. I pray this in the name of Jesus, amen.

If you genuinely and sincerely pray this prayer, as the Bible
says, you are a new creation.

> Therefore, if anyone is in Christ, he is a new creation; the old
> has gone, the new has come! (2 Corinthians 5:17)

You are now born of the Spirit of God. You have eternal life in
Christ Jesus, as the Bible says:

> I write these things to you who believe in the name of the
> Son of God so that you may know that you have eternal life.
> (1 John 5:13)

If you prayed this prayer with me, please write me a line or two by e-mail, and let me know. In the meantime, find a church that believes and teaches the whole Bible, and be part of that church. After joining the church, make sure you find a group of people with whom you can study the Word of God.

Let me leave you with this word from the Bible:

> Come, all you who are thirsty,
>   come to the waters;
> and you who have no money,
>   come, buy and eat!
> Come, buy wine and milk
>   without money and without cost.
> Why spend money on what is not bread,
>   and your labor on what does not satisfy?
> Listen, listen to me, and eat what is good,
>   and you will delight in the richest of fare. (Isaiah 55:1–2)

God calls us to a life of feasting on the best things. Sexual purity is one part of living that life. Ultimately, though, it's all about being surrendered to God in every area of our lives. I wish you all the best as you learn to walk with him!

Connect with the Author

E-mail: kifetew@yahoo.com or missysalt&light@gmail.com
Facebook: www.facebook.com/appealforpurity

For more information and resources, including a Parent Guide
to *Beyond the Fairy Tale*, and a Leader Guide for use in small
groups, visit:
www.appealforpurity.org

Acknowledgments

I would like to express my gratitude to the many people who saw me through this book; to all those who provided support, talked things over, read, wrote, offered comments, allowed me to quote their remarks, and assisted in the editing, proofreading, and designing of *Beyond the Fairy Tale*.

First and foremost, I would like to thank my kind, loving, and caring husband, Berhan, for standing beside me throughout the process of writing and publishing this book. He has been my inspiration and motivation from day one until this day. I also want to thank my wonderful children, Abel, Lydia, and Biruk, for teaching me how to laugh at my mistakes instead of pulling my hair out and for agreeing to call *Beyond the Fairy Tale* their fourth sibling.

I would like to express my appreciation to my parents and all my siblings. You have been a source of relentless courage and vitality for me throughout my life.

I'm also grateful to Bill Carmichael, for believing in me when I first contacted Deep River Books to inquire about getting my book published. He not only motivated, challenged, and inspired me to pursue my dream, but he also helped me pursue it by finding a sponsor to help with the financial aspect of the publishing process.

If it was not for my sponsor, Mrs. LeeAnn Rawlins, this book wouldn't be published. So, to LeeAnn and the whole Rawlins family, I say thank you.

I also appreciate three people from the Grace Christian Elementary School in Bowie, Maryland: Karen Cain, Rachel Duncan, and Mrs. Laura Lee Ritter, who edited and proofread the manuscript.

Last but not least, I would like to thank Rachel Starr Thomas, Robin Black, Kit Tosello, Crystal Vogt, and all the Deep River Books staff who helped me on the journey to publication.